"We serve a God who is in the business of saving people. Through his book, *What Jesus Did*, David Soesbee equips the reader to go out boldly into the world and get about the business of sharing with the lost. When you lead someone to the Lord, you don't know the great things God has planned for that life. David's passion for evangelism and his 20-plus years of experience in preaching have cumulated into this teaching, which will not only prepare you with practical skills, but will also move you to have a passion for the lost. The church needs more people who are deeply in love with Jesus and are willing to put themselves on the line to share the good news of what Jesus did."

—Dr. Johnny M. Hunt
Senior Pastor, First Baptist Woodstock, Georgia
President, Southern Baptist Convention 2008-2009

"It may sound shallow, but for me the real gem in this book is the introduction. We live in a narrative culture and the testimony that David shares-authentic and raw-is the reason that the rest of the book makes sense. While a testimony of bad behavior to redemption is not everybody's story, it is a compelling reminder that evangelism is a conversation not a program. The principles of evangelism come alive because of the stories throughout that keep the book grounded."

—Dr. R. Allen Jackson
New Orleans Baptist Theological Seminary

"Reverend Henry Maxwell asked himself, "What would Jesus do?" in Charles Sheldon's classic *In His Steps*. In *What Jesus Did* evangelist David Soesbee moves readers beyond asking speculative questions of what things Jesus would or would not do to examining what Jesus actually did—evangelism! Teeming with testimonies and saturated with Scripture, Soesbee has written a Bible study that will encourage believers and churches alike to emulate not only what Jesus did, but how Jesus did evangelism."

—MATT QUEEN, L. R. Scarborough Chair of Evangelism ("The Chair of Fire"), Assistant Professor of Evangelism, Associate Dean for Doctoral Programs, Roy Fish School of Evangelism and Missions, Southwestern Baptist Theological Seminary

"I've had the privilege of teaching *What Jesus Did* to several classes. This study encompasses what it means to live out the Great Commission in your everyday life. Not only does David teach you about relational evangelism, but he leads out by example in sharing the stories of his encounters with the lost in his own life. The underlying tone in every chapter is a constant, but subtle, reminder that you don't have to have high evangelist gifts to share your faith, but that all believers are fully equipped through the power of the Holy Spirit to lead someone to faith in Jesus Christ. I've been able to personally witness this impact on our church members' lives through *What Jesus Did*!"

—Pastor Ellis Daniel
New Hope Baptist Church, Senoia, Georgia

"David Soesbee has truly captured the essence of evangelism in this Bible study. His stories are captivating and his approach to evangelism is profound. Yet, it is written in such a practical and simple style that any follower of Jesus would be comfortable in carrying out the Great Commission. Christianity has been waiting for this approach to evangelism."

—Dr. Nathanial Hearne
President of Made Up Minds and Founder of Euless Loaves and Fishes Foundation
Author of *Friday Night Lights: Untold Stories from Behind the Lights*

Evangelism for Everyone
7 Week Study
for individuals and groups

DAVID SOESBEE

TOUCH
PUBLISHING

Copyright © 2014 by David Soesbee

ISBN: 978-0-9919839-7-1

All rights reserved. No portion of this book may be reproduced, stored in a retrieval system, or transmitted in any form or by any means—electronic, mechanical, photocopy, recording, or any other—without prior written consent from the publisher.

Scripture taken from the New American Standard Bible®. Copyright © 1960, 1962, 1963, 1968, 1971, 1972, 1973, 1975, 1977, 1995 by The Lockman Foundation. Used by permission.

Published by Touch Publishing
Requests should be directed to:
P.O. Box 541495
Grand Prairie, Texas 75054
www.TouchPublishingServices.com

To bring David Soesbee to your church, outreach, conference, or community event contact him through the publisher or through his ministry website.
www.WhatJesusDid.org

*Some of the names of the people in the personal stories have been changed for privacy protection

Cover designed by Touch Publishing
Editing by Kimberly Soesbee: www.kimberlysoesbee.com

Library of Congress Control Number: 2014939471

Printed in the United States of America on acid-free paper

DEDICATION

In memory of Dr. Randy Kilby (1955 - 1997)

I only had the chance to know Dr. Randy Kilby from 1994 to 1996, while I attended Fruitland Baptist Bible College. In that short time, he had a huge impact on my life. Dr. Kilby was the president of Fruitland, and the one thing I loved most about him was that he was very personable and a great encourager. He was quick with jokes and preached with intense passion. Dr. Kilby left a large void when he passed, but, in his little time on this earth, he left an enduring legacy. Dr. Kilby was never ashamed to bring praise to Jesus whenever possible, and he led by an example that we all should follow.

I was blessed to be able to call Dr. Randy Kilby my friend.

I dedicate this book to my beautiful wife, Kimberly. Baby, you shine brighter than the sun in the sky and always bring light to my day. Next to my salvation, you are the best gift the Lord has given to me, and He knew exactly when to bring you into my life. I love you and thank you for your overwhelming support and love for me. Thank you for being my rock. I look forward to seeing what lies ahead for us in this awesome journey the Lord has placed before us.

CONTENTS

Introduction	1
Week 1: Being an Evangelist	9
Day 1: The Problem with Evangelism	10
Day 2: Who is an Evangelist?	16
Day 3: Always Prepared	24
Day 4: Be A Spiritual Stud	30
Group Discussion	36
Week 2: What Jesus Did	37
Day 1: Jesus Gives Life	39
Day 2: Jesus Gives Passion	43
Day 3: Jesus Gives Healing	46
Day 4: Jesus Gives Love	50
Group Discussion	54
Week 3: Removing Your Barriers	55
Day 1: "I'm Afraid"	57
Day 2: "I Don't Want to Offend"	61
Day 3: "I'm Not Worthy"	64
Day 4: "I Don't Know How to Begin"	67
Group Discussion	71
Week 4: The Competition	72
Day 1: Muslim Faith	75
Day 2: Hinduism	77
Day 3: Jehovah's Witnesses	79
Day 4: Mormonism	82
Group Discussion	84

Week 5: Becoming Disciples	85
Day 1: Quick to Hear, Slow to Speak	86
Day 2: 7 Tips for Success	89
Day 3: Before, After, Still Changing	96
Day 4: Urgency and Choices	101
Group Discussion	106
Week 6: Yeah, but ...	107
Day 1: You Don't Know Bo!	109
Day 2: Not All Roads Lead to Heaven	113
Day 3: The Party's Not Over!	115
Day 4: I Knew You When	118
Group Discussion	121
Week 7: Making Disciples	122
Day 1: The Work in Progress	124
Day 2: Guiding the New Believer	128
Day 3: Be A Paul, Find A Timothy	132
Day 4: Being An Evangelist Who Leaves A Legacy	136
Group Discussion	142
Songs	143
More Stories of Salvation	145
Your Story	151
Evangelist in Progress	157
About the Author	163

INTRODUCTION

I sold my first bag of pot when I was ten years old.

You might wonder: *Who'd buy drugs from a ten year old?* Younger kids who had a buck or two to buy a joint. Older kids who wanted to smoke or take a hit of speed. People who had heard from other people that marijuana was harmless.

Next you might wonder: *What kind of ten year old would start selling drugs?* One who didn't have a positive male role model in his life. One who had been secretly abused from a young age and desperately wanted to fit in so that people would like him. You see, when I was ten, I hung out at a pool hall. I didn't have much else to do, and I liked being around guys who were bigger than me. It made me feel tough. One day, an older dude came up to me and said, "Hey kid, want to make some money?"

"Sure," my eyes lit up, "what do I have to do?"

"Take this and sell it to your friends. And don't ever tell anyone where you got it."

That's all it took. There was high demand for the stuff I had, and when you start selling so young, you become pretty good at it. It brought me great popularity as a teenager. By the time I was twenty-three, I knew I wouldn't be around to see thirty. My life was heading in one direction. I knew it. I didn't much care though. I had the confidence of Mike Tyson going up against a kindergartener. I knew my time on earth was borrowed, and I knew the man who had my soul on loan. I saw his face in the dead of night. He was the echo in the words spoken by adults who wrote me off as good-for-nothing. His was the voice in my head, telling me that my life was worthless, useless, and that the lives of those around me were just as undeserving of anything good as I was. It was at his prompting and to his good pleasure that I sold drugs, drank heavily, didn't respect women, and got into fights for no good reason.

I was headed straight to hell and didn't care when it happened.

My mom tried to keep me straight. She truly did. But as a single mother battling multiple sclerosis, and with two other kids besides me to look after, she had her hands more than full. My dad wasn't a help, and if anything, piled more grief onto my mom's already full plate. I kept my problems hidden from my mom and my siblings. I knew my mom was sick and I didn't want to worry her. I had determined that I had one person to worry about. Me. I had my first job at age eight. I smoked my first joint at age nine. And, like I said, I was selling drugs at age ten. I knew how to do whatever was necessary to exist.

I've always said I'll take street smarts over book smarts any day. Maybe I've always said that because it was my street smarts that allowed me to survive some pretty horrific things that happened during my childhood. Things that continue to haunt me when the night shadows have their way with my dreams. There are things that I will likely never forget and as hard as I've tried, I may never get over.

School was extremely difficult for me, so when my school days were done all I had left were my street smarts and some strong drug connections that allowed me to party like nobody's business on weekends, and gave me the money I needed to do what I wanted during the day.

There was a guy I knew in high school who was on a completely different path than I was. Jamie was a star athlete and an all-around nice guy who stayed out of the party scene. Jamie always had a kind word for me. He had a wide smile that was genuine. When he would tell me, "Hey, it's great to see you!" I believed he meant it.

Jamie would often invite me to church with him on Sundays. He attended the West Asheville Baptist Church, where his dad was the head pastor. Jamie wouldn't just ask me to come, though, he offered to drive me there if I needed it. I'd smile and thank him, but I never took him up on his offer. On Sundays I was too busy sleeping in and recovering from Friday and Saturday to go to church.

But one Sunday morning, when I was twenty-three years old, that changed. For several weeks I'd had a growing discomfort building up inside of me. I'd wake up after a night of drinking and doing drugs and I felt extremely unsettled. Something was missing from my life that drugs, booze, or women wouldn't fill. On this particular Sunday morning, I decided to dig out whatever best clothes I had and go to the temple. My mom had taken us to the Mormon temple when I was little, and I wondered if I'd find some sense of balance for the turmoil in my soul if I returned there.

As I got in my car, I heard a voice in my head. It was Jamie, the guy I'd known

Introduction

in high school. In my head I heard him invite me, as he'd done so many times. I knew where the West Asheville Baptist Church was located. It was closer to the tiny trailer I lived in than the Mormon temple was, so I decided to go there instead.

As I got out of my car, I was acutely aware of how I looked. My hair was long. (What can I say? It was 1989.) My clothes weren't nearly as nice as those on the people around me. And, I'd been out partying the night before, so I looked the part of a head-banger. I felt like I stuck out worse than I'd ever stuck out anywhere before. Ever.

As I walked into the back of their temple (I didn't know it was called a church), all eyes turned to me. My hair felt longer and my clothes felt rattier than they did when I was in the car. It was as if someone had scratched their nails down a chalkboard and everyone turned at once to see who did it. A few older men and women came toward me. I thought to myself, *They're gonna kick you out of here. You don't belong here.*

The tallest man in the place reached me first. He didn't hesitate to stick out his hand, look me in the eye, and declare, "Good morning! It's so great to have you here."

I shook his hand cautiously and slowly replied, "Thank you."

Then he said to me, "You're right on time. Go on in and have a seat."

I walked to the front and took a spot in the third row. There was a choir loft up on the stage, and Jamie was there. When he spotted me, he jumped over the rail and ran to me. I was a little freaked out. But he hugged me and mirrored the sentiment of the tall guy.

"It's great to have you here," he said warmly.

He returned to the choir and I sat down. The service started. We sang some songs, and then the pastor, Dr. Johnson (Jamie's dad), spoke. For forty minutes I listened intently. I realized that what went on in this temple was significantly different from what went on in the Mormon temple. This man spoke about Jesus like he was someone you could get to know intimately. In fact, the pastor seemed to know Jesus as if he were a real person that he could talk to and hear from. I tried to process how that was possible. Wasn't Jesus dead?

What was even weirder to me was that the people all around me were giving feedback to the pastor as he spoke. In the Mormon service, we sat quietly and didn't budge or give a peep. These people were shouting, "Amen" or "Thank you, Lord," and they were smiling and nodding along with what the pastor was saying.

These people were in some sort of club or allegiance together and it centered around Christ. I was fascinated. At the end of the service I watched as several people left their seats and went forward upon Dr. Johnson's invitation to "give their hearts to Jesus." He welcomed them to approach the altar boldly and ask Christ to give them a new life. Some were crying, some weren't. Some simply came to the front, kneeled, and prayed. Others came and talked to the pastor quietly, usually while dabbing their eyes.

As I watched, I thought to myself, "These people have issues."

I was in awe of what went on in this temple.

I was so taken with what went on there, that I went back the next week, and the next. In fact, for several weeks to follow my weekend routine involved parties on Friday and Saturday, and West Asheville Baptist Church on Sunday morning. The messages the pastor gave in his sermons would come back to me during the week. I thought about them when I was at work. His words reverberated in my head sometimes at night.

One Saturday morning I awoke with my mind swirling with questions. I had partied especially hard the night before and I felt terrible. I looked at the clock. It was ten o'clock in the morning. As I lay there, I wondered if God was real. I threw up a challenge to the air. I said, "God, if you're out there, I dare you to show yourself to me. Prove that you're real."

I continued to think about various things I'd heard Dr. Johnson say over the past weeks I'd been attending his church. What bothered me the most is that I couldn't figure out how Jesus fit into it all. Pressure began to build inside of me, and I felt frustrated at my confusion. I decided I would give Dr. Johnson a call, since he was the one who put all these questions in my head anyway.

I walked toward my telephone and it began to ring. I assumed it was one of my friends, calling to solidify our plans for that night. It was a Saturday, after all, so we needed to know who was going where, what drugs we needed, and what time we'd meet up. I decided to let my answering machine pick up the call. When the machine didn't pick up after its normal four rings, then five, then six, I thought with frustration that I needed to get a new machine. I let it ring eight times, then decided to answer the call, tell whoever it was that I'd call back, and then hang up quick so I could call Dr.

Introduction

Johnson.

"Hello," I said.

"Is David Soesbee there?" a male voice on the other end asked.

"This is he," I replied.

"David, this is Dr. Johnson from West Asheville Baptist Church," he said. My chest got tight, and I looked around.

Are you kidding me? I said to God.

Dr. Johnson continued, "I was praying for God to lay someone on my heart as to who I should call today, and He laid your name there. Can you come see me this afternoon?"

I went to Dr. Johnson's home for our two o'clock meeting. I was anxious to get there because the battle that was happening in my mind was unlike anything I'd ever experienced. And believe me, my mind had been through some pretty wild things.

We sat at his dining room table. I had butterflies swirling around my insides, like when you are summoned to the principal's office and aren't sure why. In the short time I'd known Dr. Johnson, I'd come to respect him greatly. It was hard not to. When he spoke, he commanded the attention of his audience simply through his presence. He carried authority with a confidence that was not arrogant, but inviting. He had qualities that I'd wished I had. I was awed at how he could be so bold while speaking to a packed church. I hated speaking in front of people so much that in high school I did not hesitate to take an F on any assignment that required me to present or read in front of the class. No questions asked, I simply wouldn't do it.

So when Dr. Johnson began explaining to me that day who Jesus Christ was and why he loved me, I listened. And when he explained why Jesus died for me, I was overwhelmed with the thought that someone would ever do something so huge for me. I knew what it meant to fight for someone else, but to have someone fight for *me*? That concept was difficult for me to grasp.

After thirty minutes or so, Dr. Johnson asked me if I wanted to accept the gift that Christ offered.

"It sounds incredible, Dr. Johnson. But, I don't think God would want someone like me," I responded. I truly could not imagine God wanting anything to do with me.

"That's the wonderful thing about God, David," Dr. Johnson replied. "He wants you exactly how you are. Right now. He just wants you to be there, and to be real."

"I don't think you understand," I explained, trying to get him to realize just how unclean I was. "I have things I need to change before I could come before God. I've done some pretty bad things."

"David, let me tell you something. There are things in your life that you want to change. Some of them, you'll be able to do on your own with a lot of work. Some things will be more of a battle–you'll struggle hard, but will get there eventually. And some things, no matter what you do, no matter how hard you try, you will never, ever change. You'll scream, you'll scratch, and you'll fight, but you'll never do it," he paused, then asked me, "Did you see the Cub Cadet riding mower in my front yard?"

"Yes, sir, I saw it," I replied.

"Do you think I could go out there, grab it, and roll it over?"

"Yes, I believe you can."

"I could. But I would struggle to do it. It would take me a few tries to flip it. If you came out there and helped me though, it would be a lot easier."

"Yeah, we could really toss that thing," I answered. "No problem at all."

Dr. Johnson leaned forward and looked at me intensely as he said, "That's what it is like when you accept Christ into your life. You no longer have to try and do things, or change things, on your own. You have the help of the most powerful man in the world."

A lightbulb turned on in my brain. Everything I was trying to figure out about why I needed Christ suddenly became illuminated through Dr. Johnson's explanation.

"I need that," I declared with a certainty I'd never had about anything before. "What do I have to do to accept Christ?"

Dr. Johnson smiled. "Pray with me," he said. "I'm going to pray, and you say the words I say. But the power isn't in these particular words. The power is in what Christ is doing in your heart. The condition of your heart is what matters most."

Dr. Johnson prayed, and I repeated what he said. But my mind was racing as I prayed. It was as if he was going too slow for me. I wanted to talk to God on my own, and let him know that I was ready for His Son, Jesus, to change me. I began to speak out the sins I'd committed. It was as if my spirit was spewing them out of my body, confessing everything I'd done that was vile and disgusting. I confessed the things I'd done against others and against God. I begged God to forgive me. Now, keep in mind, I'd done a lot of really awful things. So this process took a while. When I was done, I was crying hard. The tears and mucus that flowed from me was a catalyst. It was a release of all my sins, my pain, my anguish, and my frustrations.

I looked up at Dr. Johnson. He was crying too.

"How was that?" I asked him honestly.

"Oh, that was good," he said.

"What do I do now?"

"Now, David, you start studying and reading the word of God. And tell people what you did, and what Jesus did for you."

I stayed under the pastoral teaching of Dr. Johnson as I grew in my knowledge of Christ. Dr. Johnson was right. Changing some aspects of my behaviors and habits was difficult. But I had Christ to help me. More importantly, I was committed to allowing Him to help me. I searched out what His word instructed and I became better at learning to listen to the Holy Spirit speak to me.

A few years later, I was taking college courses to become a physical therapist. I thought that as I was helping people heal physically, I would have many open doors to talk to them about their spiritual healing. However, God had other plans. He began to show me that I was to put full-time efforts into ministering to others. This shift in focus wasn't something I entered into lightly. I told Dr. Johnson that I felt like God was calling me into a ministry of some sort. And I asked him what he thought about that.

Dr. Johnson replied, "I don't know, David, I'm not God."

I needed a little more guidance than that. He went on, "If you can do anything else, do it. But if you cannot, then don't ignore the call of God on your life."

I could not ignore the call. I enrolled in seminary to find out what God was calling me into. After seminary and interning with a large church, I knew that my calling was to evangelize. Evangelism, at that time, had a bad reputation in the public's and church's eyes, because of the scandals surrounding well-known television evangelists. I couldn't believe God was asking me to join that crowd.

But he wasn't. He was asking me to go out and preach His word to people who needed to hear it. That is evangelism. Television is but one channel where preaching God's word can take place. So if your definition of evangelism is limited to thinking only about the T.V. personalities, you need to wipe that clean from your mind.

Every one of God's children is called to evangelize. Very few do it. This study is a cumulation of my experiences over the past 20+ years as a full-time evangelist. My purpose is to help you, my brother or sister in Christ, learn that evangelizing is not something that is reserved for the guy on T.V., or for the street-corner preacher. Evangelism is a requirement of your faith. And it isn't mysterious, it doesn't take any special training, and it's not something to be afraid of.

I invite you to join me on a journey to a deeper understanding of what Jesus did for you, and show you how easy it is to share that good news with the world.

WEEK ONE
BEING AN EVANGELIST

Before we dive into our first week of study, I want to explain how this book is organized, and how you can make the most of it.

Over the next seven weeks, my goal is to equip you and motivate you to go into the world and share what Jesus did for you, and for every person on this earth. My sincere prayer is that you will not see evangelism as one more item on your already long "to-do" list, but your gratitude for what Jesus did for you will be so strong that you will be bursting to share it with others.

Each week of study includes four shorter lessons, which I've broken into days. I am hopeful that within a week's time, you can find four days to set aside an hour to grow in your knowledge of God's word. At the end of each week's materials are a set of group discussion questions. If you are engaging in this study as part of your small group, or you have a prayer partner or friend to do this study with, you can go over these questions together each week.

Along the outer column of each page are various items that will enhance your study. This includes things like relevant Scriptures to memorize,

> Then He said to His disciples, "The harvest is plentiful, but the workers are few. Therefore beseech the Lord of the harvest to send out workers into His harvest."
> Matthew 9:37-38

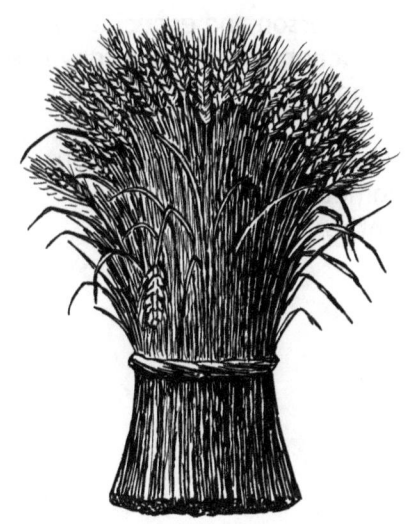

questions for further reflection, and items to add to your evangelism toolbox that will make your study time even stronger. As you work, you'll need this book, a Bible, a pen, and always begin with prayer.

DAY ONE - THE PROBLEM WITH EVANGELISM

Evangelism
noun \i-van-jə-li-zəm\

1. the winning or revival of personal commitments to Christ

2. militant or crusading zeal

Evangelist
noun \i-van-jə-list\

1. a person and especially a preacher who tries to convince people to become Christian

2. someone who talks about something with great enthusiasm

Over the years, countless programs and studies have been written on evangelism. Evangelism is taught through church classes, in books, at workshops, and in seminary courses. Nearly all of the evangelism "how-to" material that I've encountered (I've seen more than 100 different evangelism approaches presented, in addition to taking evangelism courses at seminary) teach that evangelizing is best accomplished when one first memorizes a series of Bible verses, or even entire biblical passages, and then presents those verses in an orderly way to the non-believer.

There are indeed many good books out there about evangelism. But when it comes right down to it, the frustration I have is that formulated processes that call on you to memorize and regurgitate Scripture in order to lead someone to Christ have created a major problem within the church. Your average, Bible-believing, Jesus-following Christian claims they don't evangelize for one of two reasons:

1. They don't feel they know **enough** Scripture
2. They feel they don't know the **right** Scripture

Evangelism studies and programs have

complicated things to the point where people feel they have to be a seminary scholar in order to do this thing called evangelism.

I'm not saying that learning Scriptures is not important and necessary for a Christian. A man I greatly respect, Dr. Charles Swindoll, wrote: "I know of no other single practice in the Christian life more rewarding, practically speaking, than memorizing Scripture ... No other single exercise pays greater spiritual dividends! Your prayer life will be strengthened. Your witnessing will be sharper and much more effective. Your attitudes and outlook will begin to change. Your mind will become alert and observant. Your confidence and assurance will be enhanced. Your faith will be solidified."

Every area of your life with Christ is enhanced when you commit God's word to your memory. The greatest benefits to memorizing Scripture are reserved for YOU! If you wait around until you know every verse in proper order before you will share your faith and lead someone to the Lord, believe me when I say, you'll never feel ready.

1. Read the following verses. Circle the reason that each verse states as to why God's word is important.

Your word I have treasured in my heart, That I may not sin against You. (Psalm 119:11)

All Scripture is inspired by God and profitable for teaching, for reproof, for correction, for training in righteousness; (2 Timothy 3:16)

Is it being said, O house of Jacob: 'Is the Spirit of the LORD impatient? Are these His doings?' Do not My words do good to the one walking uprightly? (Micah 2:7)

This book of the law shall not depart from your mouth, but you shall meditate on it day and night, so that you may be careful to do according to all that is written in it; for then you will make your way prosperous, and then you will have success. (Joshua 1:8)

Your word is a lamp to my feet and a light to my path.
Psalm 119:105

In reading these verses, I trust you can see that they are not written to unbelievers. They are written to God's children. God's word is critical to us, the followers of Jesus, as the very thing that will keep us on His path and guide us away from sin.

I think that although Christians claim they feel inadequate when it comes to sharing their faith, the reason many Christians don't evangelize runs a little deeper. Less than one fifth of those who call themselves Christians actually hold a true biblical worldview. A biblical worldview means that one uses the Bible as the lens through which all decisions are made. It means one believes that the Bible is completely accurate, and holds the answers for all questions related to moral beliefs and actions. So, four out of every five Christians *don't* believe the Bible to be fully relevant for making decisions as to how they should live their life.

2. Have you ever stopped to consider your worldview? If not, now is the time! If you say that you hold a biblical worldview, take a moment and ask God to reveal to you if that is true. Does the lifestyle you lead align with the truths God presents in His word?

Week 1: Being an Evangelist

More and more believers are using the Scriptures as a buffet to pick and choose what they want to make it right for them. This is true in our daily life and it is true when it comes to evangelism. Too many Christians make Scriptures conform to what they want to believe rather than taking the Scriptures literally and conforming their actions to what the Bible teaches.

That is important to note as we begin our study of evangelism, because if you are among those who say you follow Christ, but don't take the Bible seriously in *your* lifestyle, how can you expect the non-believer to remotely believe any Scripture that you throw at them?

Professing faith in Christ and living as such are two different things. The person to whom you evangelize will undoubtedly take notice of your own actions and will align them to what they perceive a "Christian" should be. If you are not living what you profess to believe, the non-believer will see it. He or she may even call you out on it. Especially if your method of evangelizing is to hit them up with Scriptures that you are not even living out.

The problem with evangelism today isn't the message itself. The problem is that the messengers are not passionate about what they believe nor are they willing to do the hard work of living out their faith boldly.

This may sound like a harsh word, but if you truly are using this resource with the goal of becoming better at sharing your faith, then you need to ensure that your thinking about God's word aligns with His. He intends us to live by His word. He intends us to acknowledge Him in all our ways.

We are not to be wreckless and careless with

- † 95% of Christians have never led someone into a saving relationship with Christ
- † 80% of Christians do not consistently witness for Christ
- † 100% of Christians in Evangelical denominations believe they should share their faith
- † About 2.6 billion people in the world have heard the gospel, but have not accepted Christ
- † About 3.5 billion people in the world have not yet heard the gospel directly

"For My thoughts are not your thoughts,
Nor are your ways My ways," declares the Lord.
"For as the heavens are higher than the earth,
So are My ways higher than your ways
And My thoughts than your thoughts.
For as the rain and the snow come down from heaven,
And do not return there without watering the earth
And making it bear and sprout,
And furnishing seed to the sower and bread to the eater;
So will My word be which goes forth from My mouth;
It will not return to Me empty,
Without accomplishing what I desire,
And without succeeding in the matter for which I sent it."
                    Isaiah 55:8-11

God's word. That is one of my main concerns with people who learn the standard "evangelizing" Scriptures and then spout them off in hopes that the other person will see the error in his ways and accept Christ. Scriptures are not platitudes or fortune cookie "good wishes." They were spoken from the mouth of a Holy God.

I have heard dozens of believers jump into quoting Scripture wrecklessly with someone they are trying to evangelize to. In doing so, they build a wall that prevents the other person from truly hearing them.

Even worse, if you are quoting Scripture when you aren't even 100% convinced Scripture is absolute truth, you will be recognized for your hypocrisy and your evangelism efforts will be ineffective.

"But," you say, "the Bible tells us that God's word will not return void, so even if I don't believe some of the parts of the Bible, isn't quoting some Scripture better than anything else?"

That thinking is rooted from Isaiah 55. Look at the verses listed along the left and circle the pronouns.

3. Who is speaking in this passage?

4. Who is sending forth the words being spoken?

5. From whose mouth do the words come?

This passage of Scripture is referring to God's sovereignty over everything. It teaches us that God is in control over this world. His plans, which we cannot begin to formulate ourselves, will always be fulfilled. He speaks. It happens.

The passage does not say, "When David speaks, God makes it happen." Do you see the difference? We must treat God's word with respect. We cannot throw it around and assume God will work everything out.

"So," you might be saying now, "if you are telling me that I shouldn't quote Scripture verses when I evangelize, what are you telling me to do?"

I'm glad you asked.

In this book, we will study Scripture for the purpose of building <u>you</u> in your faith. For the purpose of deepening <u>your</u> understanding of who God is. For the purpose of allowing the Holy Spirit opportunities to reveal new and fresh truths to <u>you</u>.

A study by LifeWay revealed that nearly 82% of church-going Christians do NOT touch their Bible every day. So I want to exhort you to get into God's word for <u>you</u>. Then, and only then, will you be equipped to evangelize with others.

What we *are* going to do is deepen your understanding of what Jesus did for you and prepare you to have such confidence and excitement in how Jesus changed your life that you will not be able to contain yourself from sharing it with the world.

My prayer for you ...

God, I pray that whoever is engaged in this study today will have a burning desire in their heart to hear what you have to say to them about evangelism.

If there are areas he or she needs to get right with you, I pray you call those to mind and bring a spirit of repentance, so we can move forward victoriously and fully committed to that which you've called us to do.

DAY TWO - WHO IS AN EVANGELIST?

1. Without looking up any information online, in a dictionary, or in any book, write down your definition of what an evangelist is and what an evangelist does.

Journaling

When is the last time you would say you "evangelized"?

What were the circumstances?

What was the result?

Recall as much as you can from that day. Write it down as if you were writing a story for someone else to read. Then, as you reflect, ask God to reveal new truths to you about your evangelism efforts.

One morning our Sunday school class began discussing how we should evangelize with our neighbors and coworkers. I was dismayed when the majority of the responses my fellow believers gave included things like:

"They all know I go to church."

"I try and and be a good example."

"I do extra things for my neighbor, like mowing her yard."

"I try and stand out by parenting my kids differently."

"My coworkers know I won't go out to happy hour or to the clubs after work."

These are all positive things. But can they be called *evangelism*?

Read the biblical definition of evangelism given on the right of the next page. Highlight or circle what evangelism means.

In day one's study, I made the claim that I believe one reason people don't evangelize is that evangelism programs have complicated things so much that people feel they either don't know enough Scripture or the proper Scriptures. I also said that I think simply using Scriptures in evangelism is not enough because people aren't studying Scripture at a deep enough level themselves, or they aren't fully committed to Scripture as THE guiding light for their life. I pray if that is you, then you will commit yourself to a renewed faith in God's word as truth for your life.

But I also think the reason many Christians don't evangelize is they don't see themselves as an evangelist. Many Christians have relegated the task of evangelism to those preachers who are called into full-time Christian evangelical ministry. I'm going to make a bold statement that you might initially disagree with, but stay with me: We are **all** called to be evangelists.

You can see from the translation of the Greek words to the right that evangelism means to 'bring good news.'

A Biblical Definition:

The English word Evangelism is derived from the Greek word 'euaggelion' which, literally translated in the noun form means 'gospel' or 'good news.'

When put into verb form, (euaggelizesthiai) the meaning of the word has a slight change to mean 'announce' or 'bring good news.'

The Greek word in its various forms appears fifty-five times in the New Testament. With the many different forms of translation, the Greek word can also be translated as 'preach.'

And He (Jesus) said to them, "Go into all the world and preach the gospel (good news) to all creation." (Mark 16:15)

This verse is from Mark's accounting of Jesus's final instructions before He physically departed earth. It is definitely an instruction to preach the good news. But was that instruction only for the disciples of that time?

I believe not.

But you are a chosen race, a royal priesthood, a holy nation, a people for God's own possession, so that you may proclaim the excellencies of Him who has called you out of darkness into His marvelous light. (1 Peter 2:9)

2. According to this verse, what are God's chosen people to do?

God called us out of darkness for a reason. That reason is to proclaim who He is to other people. This means more than sitting around with your Christian friends and talking about how great God is. Yes, we should meet together and build our brothers and sisters in Christ up with our praise stories. But God has more in mind.

Go therefore and make disciples of all the nations, baptizing them in the name of the Father and the Son and the Holy Spirit, teaching them to observe all that I commanded you; and lo, I am with you always, even to the end of the age. (Matthew 28:19-20)

3. Circle or highlight the verbs in the above passage.

4. What are Jesus's followers called to do?

5. To whom are they called to do it?

Week 1: Being an Evangelist

In Matthew's account of Jesus's last words, we're shown that we are to not only to proclaim the words of the good news, but we are all to **make disciples**. In order to make a disciple, we have to give someone the opportunity to **become** a disciple.

Someone will not make the decision to follow Christ if they are never given the chance to make that decision.

Romans 10:13-15 - For, "Everyone who calls on the name of the Lord will be saved." How, then, can they call on the one they have not believed in? And how can they believe in the one of whom they have not heard? And how can they hear without someone preaching to them? And how can anyone preach unless they are sent? As it is written: "How beautiful are the feet of those who bring good news!"

6. Sum up these verses in your own words.

SALVATION CAN BEGIN WHEN SOMEONE BRINGS THE GOOD NEWS. THOSE WHO BRING THE GOOD NEWS ARE BEAUTIFUL!

Can you see the process Paul follows? If you back it up from the end of the verse to the beginning you see:

1. The good news is preached
2. Someone hears it
3. That person believes it
4. They call on the name of the Lord
5. That person is saved

Salvation begins with the bringing of the good news. It is available to everyone. Therefore, none of us are exempt from bringing that good news, because "everyone" is all around us.

I said this earlier, but I don't want you to miss it: In order for us, the followers of Christ, to fulfill Jesus's command to "make disciples" we must give people the opportunity to become disciples.

Let me be clear on something. There are those, like myself, who are called by God as evangelists as our vocation. We intentionally pursue ministerial opportunities to go out and preach, teach, and present the gospel message intentionally for the purpose of winning lost souls to Christ.

But the fact that some people evangelize as a full-time pursuit does not let every other believer in Christ off the hook for taking the opportunity to present the gospel message when God places someone before them who needs to hear it.

Living a good life, raising your kids to have strong morals, helping your neighbor, going to church–these are all important as you live out what the Bible teaches. I spoke of that in the previous lesson. Our walk must match our talk. A walk that doesn't match the talk will be noticed by the non-believers and can hinder them in hearing the good news. BUT, if doing good deeds is the *only* thing you do, and you are calling it evangelism, then you are missing something. You are missing giving your friends and neighbors the chance to **become** disciples.

What did Jesus mean?

When Jesus said, "Go," He knew we all wouldn't GO overseas or to foreign lands to preach the gospel.

But every day, every one of us has a "Go" moment. It's that moment when you open your eyes, climb out of bed, and enter into the beauty of the day God's given you.

THAT is your "Go" moment. And when you "Go," do so with open eyes for the opportunity to make disciples of those God places in your path.

GAYLA'S STORY

During seminary, I was an intern at West Asheville Baptist Church. One day, Dr. Johnson came into my little office. He had received a phone call from a woman who requested for a pastor to come and visit her. As Dr. Johnson put it, she was a "streetwise female." He told me, "Since you came from the streets, David, I want you to go and talk to her."

I asked my friend Dickie Green, who worked for the Asheville Police Department, to come with me. She lived about 8 miles from the church. When the door opened, before us stood a tiny little woman, wearing a robe. As soon as I saw her, my first thought was that she looked like someone who would be a prostitute. I introduced Dickie and I and confirmed that she had asked for a pastor to visit her.

"Yes, yes," she replied. "Can you follow me back to my bedroom?"

Dickie and I looked at one another with raised eyebrows, but we followed her. She indicated two seats for us and she sat on her bed. She explained to us that she had been diagnosed with terminal, inoperable cancer. She was going to die. She began to cry as she explained that she didn't want God to be mad at her. She wanted to make a decision to accept Jesus as her Lord, but was afraid God wouldn't accept her because she was only feeling this prompting because she knew her days were numbered.

I asked her, "What exactly is it that you feel would keep you from receiving God's grace?"

She told us that she had been a prostitute for more than thirty years. As she explained with colorful language the extent to which she gave her body away in the past, her sobbing continued even harder.

"Have you ever prayed to receive Christ into your life?" I asked.

"No," she said sadly. "I grew up in and out of churches as a child, but it never meant anything to me."

"Gayla, why did you call our church?" I wondered. Because in the 8 mile drive from our church to her house, we passed several other churches.

"The reason I called your church," she said, "is because I used to live in the house directly across the street from it."

I knew the house she referred to because our church had purchased that land a few years back and tore down that house, making the area into a parking lot. There had been a psychic who ran a business from the first floor, and the second floor had rooms that were rented weekly to people of ill repute.

She said her bedroom window there had faced the street out front and she could see the church. She said she would often sit in the window and look out at the people arriving at the church dressed for weddings or Sunday services. She'd notice their beautiful clothes and laughter. She said she always wanted to come over there.

I looked at her and said, "But you could have."

A huge tear ran down her face as she said, "No, I couldn't. They don't want someone like me."

My heart physically ached in my chest. I realized there was some truth to her words. I also recognized my own failure in that I had never walked the two hundred steps from the front door of our church to that house and said, "We would love you to come and be a part of our fellowship."

Personally, in that moment, I knew that no one should be excluded from evangelism. I looked at her and asked her if she would like to receive the free gift of salvation that Jesus offers through accepting Him as her Lord and Savior.

"God understands your heart right now," I explained. "He knows you are going to die. He always knew you were going to die. He also knew that Dickie and I would be sitting here today talking to you."

I then shared some of my own personal testimony with her. I told her that Jesus's blood was shed for her, just as it was for me, to cover the ugliness of the sin in our lives. I wanted to reassure her that Jesus loved her first, before she was ever even born. He loved her before she made her life choices, and He loved her right then.

I asked again if she wanted to accept Christ. With a small smile that shone through her tears, she said yes. Dickie, Gayla, and I held hands as she prayed to receive Jesus Christ as her Lord. I stressed to her that it was the condition of her heart, more so than any specific words she said, that God saw.

Gayla asked if she could give us a hug. I replied, "Yes. It's always great to hug a new sister in Christ."

As she hugged Dickie, she fell back into the bed, weak from her sickness. She began to cry again and said she felt sad that Jesus had done so much for her, but she would never be able to do anything for Him.

I asked her what she meant by that. She said she wished she'd have time to tell people about what she'd done.

I smiled at her and said, "You're not dead, yet. You can start with the people closest to you. Tell them what Jesus did for you."

I left her with about fifty tracts that I had in my car. I told her she could use them to help explain what Jesus did for her. I told her to call me when she needed more.

Six days later, I received a phone call with the news that she'd been admitted into hospice. I went to visit her. When I walked in, Gayla smiled so brightly it lit the room.

"I'm so glad you're here," she said. "Do you have any more tracts? I've given all mine away."

She gave those tracts to nurses, doctors, friends, strangers–anyone who would stop and listen. I gave her another stack that I'd brought with me. We sat near her window, which was open, and visited. As people walked by she would yell out the window, "Hey! Come here! I've got something for you!" And she would give them one of the tracts. Her window faced the street, and I couldn't help but think how very different she was now, looking out this window, than she was at the window when she watched the happy church-goers of West Asheville Baptist Church all those years ago.

Gayla was not slothful or lazy in her evangelism efforts in the days God gave her from the moment of her salvation until the day she died.

My prayer for each person reading this is that you will respond to God's prompting. Since the day of your salvation, He has been calling you to go and share the good news. I pray you will recognize that we don't know how many days we have left, so we must make the most of each moment given to us to share what Jesus did in our lives.

What Jesus Did Bible Study ✡ David Soesbee

DAY THREE - ALWAYS PREPARED

Devote yourselves to prayer, being watchful and thankful. And pray for us, too, that God may open a door for our message, so that we may proclaim the mystery of Christ, for which I am in chains. Pray that I may proclaim it clearly, as I should. Be wise in the way you act toward outsiders; make the most of every opportunity. Let your conversation be always full of grace, seasoned with salt, so that you may know how to answer everyone.

Colossians 4:2-6

The United States of America has the greatest Armed Forces in the world. I say this with absolute conviction for the simple reason that I know many, many men and women who have served. And they are some of the greatest friends a person could ask for. Growing up I had a friend named TJ. TJ was one of the biggest cry-babies you ever met. He complained, he whined, and bawled at the drop of a hat. His dad forced him to play football in an effort to toughen him up.

After graduation, I learned that TJ joined the Marines and was heading off to bootcamp. I laughed. "That kid's gonna be mush," I thought. TJ went away. When he returned from bootcamp, I would have sworn I was looking at a completely different person. This young, noodle of a kid was now a man. He carried himself differently. He held a confidence I'd never seen before. He was a soldier in every sense of the word.

TJ was occasionally sent on black ops missions. Because I was clergy, he could share things with me about his activities that his family didn't know. Prior to one such mission he said to me, "I know there is a strong chance I will be killed on this trip." He knew the risks. He knew what was on the line. But he was more concerned with the well-being of those in his country than he was for his personal well-being. *Semper Paratus. Semper Fidelis.* That means: Always Prepared. Always

Week 1: Being an Evangelist

Faithful.

Before you accepted Christ, you were like TJ was before bootcamp. A wet noodle. A spiritual wimp. When the Holy Spirit came to dwell in you at your salvation you became like TJ was after bootcamp. A soldier. You now have power and strength you did not previously possess. And your motto is to be *Semper Paratus. Semper Fidelis.* Always prepared for what God puts before you. Always faithful to share the good news.

1. Make a list of all the places you feel evangelism should take place.

2. Why do you feel these are good places to evangelize?

The answer to question 1 is actually very short. It should be "anywhere I am." You see, you don't know when God will put someone before you to whom He wants you to intentionally share the gospel.

Preach the word; be ready in season and out of season; reprove, rebuke, exhort, with great patience and instruction. (2 Timothy 4:2)

3. Circle the verbs that Paul wrote to Timothy in the above verse.

4. Right now, do you consider yourself always prepared and ready, no matter what the season, to preach the word? Why or why not?

5. Whether you are prepared right now or not, what should you be doing so that you can be ready?

    I was tempted to break into a little bit of a Dr. Seuss-type rhyme here to illustrate to you all the places that evangelism can take place. "In a boat, on a plane, at the school, on a train..." Because a believer must always be ready to declare what God has done in our life.
    God gives us instruction as to *how* we are to conduct ourselves as we share.

6. Look back at 2 Timothy 4:2. How does Paul write that we are to preach the word? (Hint, it's the last four words in the verse)

7. On page 24, I listed Colossians 4:2-6. Look back to it and write below how you are to act toward outsiders, and how you should conduct conversations with them.

Week 1: Being an Evangelist

No doubt you've heard the reference to salt Jesus makes in the Sermon on the Mount, where He instructs us to be "salt and light" in our dark world. Now we read about salt again in Colossians. (Refer to the verse on page 24) Why? Salt was used as a preservative in those times because it kept food from decaying. In fact, salt was so valuable, it was even used as currency. Which, by the way, is where the term "He's not worth his salt" came from. It means someone is not measuring up to what they should be worth.

In Colossians, when Paul tells us to season our conversations with salt, I believe he wants us to talk to non-believers in such a way that we are speaking valuable words, spicy to the ears, and that they are words that will help preserve the one hearing them. Words of life.

When Jesus tells us to "be salt" He wants us to make an impact on those around us. Have you ever noticed how salt tends to permeate into whatever it comes in contact with? You can't "undo" salting something. Once it's salted, it's salted. If you add salt to your spaghetti sauce, then decide you don't want salt in there, too bad! It's not coming out.

Let the words you say be words that will last.

> The average person does not realize how important salt is to the body. It helps keep us alive. Salt runs through your blood, and if there is any great deviation from the ideal amounts, you can become seriously ill, even to the point of death.
>
> Salt helps sustain life. Can you see why Jesus used salt as an illustration for us?

8. Think back to the last conversation you had with a non-believer that you felt was "full of salt." Where were you? What prompted you to make your conversation salty?

JONATHAN'S STORY

The Texas State Fair is an event I think everyone should attend at least once in their lifetime. It is loaded with fun and you will leave there full of bacon dogs, cotton candy, and funnel cake. Yum! Businesses set up booths and displays, often with freebies that make it worth your while to stop and chat. At the Texas State Fair last year, my wife and I were lured to attend a vacation time share presentation with the promise of a $50 restaurant gift card and 2 free nights in a hotel if we sat through the whole presentation.

We arrived at the presentation excited to get our gift cards, hear the spiel, and leave with no further investment in their product. I basically told the young presenter Jonathan as much when he introduced himself to us.

"Yes sir, but we need to go through the presentation anyway," Jonathan said.

We enjoyed getting to know a bit more about Jonathan as he led us through the next ninety minutes, during which he explained benefits of purchasing a vacation property through this company. He showed us pictures, walked us through a model of the condo we would be getting, and played a video that included many happy couples enjoying "life to the fullest" on their dream vacations. My wife and I asked young Jonathan about his own travel experiences, asked him how long he'd been working for the company, and other "getting to know you" questions as we went along.

After the model home tour, Jonathan brought us into a large room filled with small, round, cafe-style tables. There must have been 75 or more tables in this room. At each one sat one of the presenters and a couple that looked much like my wife and I, ready to get their gift cards and scoot out of there. Everyone was talking, as the presenters each did their very best to convince the tired couples that spending $45,000 on a shared vacation home was actually going to *save* them money somewhere along the way.

Jonathan tried to work the numbers and switch it up every which way to get Kim and I to open our checkbook and commit to buying a time share. We remained patient and relaxed as we told him each time, "Thanks, but we really can't afford it."

After bringing over his manager for a last-ditch effort yielded no result, Jonathan was ready to let us go with our prized gift cards. But before he did, I suddenly felt prompted to speak to him about something.

"Jonathan," I began, "for the past hour and a half, you've been trying to sell us on this time share. You were doing your job. Can I ask for five more minutes of your time so I could do my job?"

"Yes sir," Jonathan replied hesitantly.

"Do you attend church?" I asked. He said yes, and told us which church he went to. It is actually one of the largest churches in the Dallas / Ft. Worth area. When I heard the name of the church, I could have ended the conversation. Often we assume that because someone goes to church, they are a follower of Christ. But my experience has taught me that is a risky assumption to make.

"When did you accept Christ?" I asked.

"Well, I've been in church all my life," Jonathan said. He seemed unsure what I was asking.

"But going to church doesn't mean you are going to heaven," I said. "Just because I stand in the middle of McDonald's, that doesn't make me a cheeseburger."

This made Jonathan laugh. I proceeded to explain to him that every person must have a moment in which they make the decision to ask Jesus Christ to come into their life and be their Lord and Savior. Each person must have a time when they recognize their sin before God, and ask for His forgiveness.

Jonathan, who attended this megachurch for his whole life, had never done that.

At that moment, in the room full of more than 200 people, who were all listening to time share presentations, the three of us held hands around our small table and Jonathan committed his life to Christ.

Jonathan's manager came over to us somewhere along the course of the conversation. He said he was a believer and he was thrilled that his employee got saved that day.

"You see," I said to the manager, "your field is ripe, right here at work."

When my wife and I went to that presentation, we did so with no more intention of anything noteworthy happening other than receiving our gift cards. Because we were sensitive to the Holy Spirit, we were patient and graceful in our speech to Jonathan, and we were prepared for the moment when it came, a young man got saved that day.

DAY FOUR - BE A SPIRITUAL STUD

> In the New Testament, the Greek word sōzō is translated as meaning
> 1. to save, keep safe and sound, to rescue from danger or destruction
> 2. to preserve one who is in danger
> 3. to deliver from the consequences of sin

After that day when I accepted Christ in Dr. Johnson's dining room, I was so pumped up I wanted to share it with someone. I called one of the guys that I frequently hung out with.

"Man, guess what just happened to me," I said.

"What?" he asked.

"I just got saved!" I told him with great excitement in my voice.

"Saved?" he said, confused. "Saved from what?"

I paused and thought about that. "I guess, I got saved from myself," I answered.

"What?"

"I have been saved from my own destruction. I accepted Jesus as my savior today."

My friend thought I was high on something. And I suppose I was. I was high on Jesus's love for me.

1. Not including whoever was present at the time, who was the first person you told about the decision you made for following Christ? If you accepted Christ as a young child, then you may not remember. But who is the first person you can remember sharing your faith with?

Look at the name that you wrote down in that first question. That person right there is the first person you evangelized to. I hope that fills you with a sense of excitement. Evangelism is telling others what Jesus did for you. It is declaring, "I was lost, but NOW! Now, I am found."

Evangelism is not a complicated process. You don't need to be a PhD or have seminary courses under your belt. What you do need is one simple thing: the Holy Spirit in you.

The most powerful tool in your evangelism toolkit is the presence of the Holy Spirit. Any evangelist that is worth his or her salt will draw from Christ's power source. We can not evangelize in our own strength or power. We need Jesus's help. He gives that help through His Helper, the Holy Spirit.

I'd like you to take some focused time to read the following passage. It is Acts 9:1-22. We will refer back to this passage later in this study, so you might want to dog-ear the page.

> But you will receive power when the Holy Spirit comes on you; and you will be my witnesses in Jerusalem, and in all Judea and Samaria, and to the ends of the earth.
>
> Acts 1:8

1 Now Saul, still breathing threats and murder against the disciples of the Lord, went to the high priest, 2 and asked for letters from him to the synagogues at Damascus, so that if he found any belonging to the Way, both men and women, he might bring them bound to Jerusalem. 3 As he was traveling, it happened that he was approaching Damascus, and suddenly a light from heaven flashed around him; 4 and he fell to the ground and heard a voice saying to him, "Saul, Saul, why are you persecuting Me?"

5 And he said, "Who are You, Lord?" And He said, "I am Jesus whom you are persecuting, 6 but get up and enter the city, and it will be told you what you must do." 7 The men who traveled with him stood speechless, hearing the voice but seeing no one. 8 Saul got up from the ground, and though his eyes were open, he could see nothing; and leading him by the hand, they brought him into Damascus. 9 And he was three days without sight, and neither ate nor drank.

10 Now there was a disciple at Damascus named Ananias; and the Lord said to him in a vision, "Ananias." And he said, "Here I am, Lord." 11 And the Lord said to him, "Get up and go to the street called Straight, and inquire at the house of Judas for a man from Tarsus named Saul, for he is praying, 12 and he has seen in a vision a man named Ananias come in and lay his hands on him, so that he might regain his sight."

13 But Ananias answered, "Lord, I have heard from many about this man, how much harm he did to Your saints at Jerusalem; 14 and here he has authority from the chief priests to bind all who call on Your name." 15 But the Lord said to him, "Go, for he is a chosen instrument of Mine, to bear My name before the Gentiles and kings and the sons of Israel; 16 for I will show him how much he must suffer for My name's sake." 17 So Ananias departed and entered the house, and after laying his hands on him said, "Brother Saul, the Lord Jesus, who appeared to you on the road by which you were coming, has sent me so that you may regain your sight and be filled with the Holy Spirit." 18 And immediately there fell from his eyes something like scales, and he regained his sight, and he got up and was baptized; 19 and he took food and was strengthened.

Now for several days he was with the disciples who were at Damascus, 20 and immediately he began to proclaim Jesus in the synagogues, saying, "He is the Son of God." 21 All those hearing him continued to be amazed, and were saying, "Is this not he who in Jerusalem destroyed those who called on this name, and who had come here for the purpose of bringing them bound before the chief priests?"

22 But Saul kept increasing in strength and confounding the Jews who lived at Damascus by proving that this Jesus is the Christ.

2. What was Saul's feeling toward Christians before his encounter on the road?

3. What did Saul claim about Jesus in verse 20?

4. How did the people who knew Saul react when they saw him after his encounter with Christ? (verse 21)

5. Where do we read that Saul first began to proclaim who Jesus was?

If there is anyone with a more dramatic story in the Bible than Saul of how someone came to know the reality of who Christ is, I'm not sure who that would be. Saul went from being a murdering, hateful, venomous man to being someone who was willing to do whatever he had to do in order to let people know that Jesus was the Son of God.

Between the time of his encounter with Jesus on the road to Damascus and the moment of his beheading, God gave him approximately 30 years to evangelize. He truly made every moment of those 30 years count. I consider Paul (Saul's new name following his conversion to Christianity) to be a spiritual stud. His evangelistic efforts are, in my opinion, unmatched.

Verse 22 of the above passage tells us, "Saul kept increasing in strength." In the Philippians passage to the right, circle the word "it." The "it" that Paul is speaking of is perfection or total conformation to who Christ is. Paul knew he was a work in progress, still changing into what Christ wanted him to be, but he kept his eye on the goal.

Like Paul, if you are saved, you have a before, after, and still changing story. To be an effective evangelist, you need to know and be able to communicate your unique story. You have to know who

> I do not regard myself as having laid hold of it yet; but one thing I do: forgetting what lies behind and reaching forward to what lies ahead, I press on toward the goal for the prize of the upward call of God in Christ Jesus.
>
> Philippians 3:13-14

What Jesus Did evangelism essentials:

1. Understand what Jesus did for you, and for every person on this earth.
2. Know your before, after, and still changing story.
3. Pray continually.
4. Remain grounded in God's word.
5. Ask God to show you who is placed before you in order for you to share the good news.

you were before Christ entered your life. You have to have that moment of conversion, and you have to be able to recognize the areas where God is still at work in you.

Your story, combined with Christ's power, is the one thing that no one can take away from you. I am going to help you recognize and be able to articulate these parts of your story as we continue through the next weeks of this study. As we do this, we will turn to Scripture to build you up in the word of God. Storehousing God's word in your heart is critical, for the Holy Spirit will bring it to mind when you need it most. Throughout these weeks I will also share with you the most common objections I've encountered as I've evangelized in 51 countries over the past 20+ years. I pray that as you read my personal stories, you will find something from each one that you can take away and tuck into your evangelism arsenal.

In Acts 1:8, Jesus tells the disciples that they will receive the power to witness to others when the Holy Spirit comes upon them. The Holy Spirit is given to those who call upon the name of Jesus as their Lord and Savior. Jesus Christ is the Son of God. He was crucified, died, and rose from the dead in order to break down the barrier between sinful mankind and our righteous, sovereign God. Those who believe this, and ask for forgiveness of sins through Christ's atoning sacrifice, are saved from eternal hell. Those who do not, will be cast into the lake of fire for eternity. Salvation is for anyone who will call upon Christ to be saved.

If you believe this in your heart, you have been given the gift of the Holy Spirit as your Helper. He will teach, rebuke, guide, and empower you to be a witness for Christ. If you have reached this point in the study and you have not ever had that moment where you decided to give your life to Christ, before we go on, I'd like to ask you one question: Will you accept the free gift of salvation that Jesus Christ offers to you?

God knows your heart. You're not able to hide the truth of whether or not you have a personal relationship with Him. If you realize right now that the reason you might not be able

Week 1: Being an Evangelist

to share your faith effectively is because you have never truly called upon Jesus to be your Lord and Savior, now is the time to get your life and your heart right with Jesus.

It is not about the words you speak, but the condition of your heart.

If this is your desire, I invite you to pray this prayer right now, inviting Christ into your life.

Jesus, I call upon you right now. I need you. Thank you, Jesus for dying on the cross for my sins. I open my heart's door to you. Lord, please come in and be Lord and Savior of my life. Thank you, Jesus for forgiving me of my sins and for giving me the free gift of eternal salvation. Jesus, I ask you to please come and take control of the throne of my life. Lord, make me and mold me into the person you want me to be. Amen.

If you prayed this prayer, you have been saved. Go and tell someone. And don't stop. You have joined the army. From this day forward you are called to go into your world and share what Jesus did for you.

Questions for Group Discussion:

Always begin your small group time with prayer.

1. What evangelism programs or tracts have you used in the past to help you share your faith with someone else? Were they effective for you? Why or why not?

2. Who was the first person that you evangelized to? (The first person you remember telling about your decision to follow Jesus)

3. How did that first person react to your news? In my life, that first friend I told eventually pulled away from me completely. He wanted nothing to do with my newfound hope. What was your experience?

4. Have someone in the group read Gayla's story out loud. Then answer the next question.

5. Gayla's house was right across the street from the church. Yet, no one ever stopped in to say hello. Is there a "Gayla's house" in your world? A person or a place where God might be prompting you to go and introduce yourself, but you've been reluctant to go?

WEEK TWO
WHAT JESUS DID

In 1897 a man named Charles Sheldon released a piece of writing that, over the years, has been read an estimated 15 million times. It was the very first entry in *100 Christian Books That Changed the Century* (by William J. and Randy Peterson). The book I am referring to is called *In His Steps*. The main character in this book, Reverend Henry Maxwell, puts a challenge out to his congregation. He wants to gain a deeper understanding of what it truly means to follow in Christ's steps. He wonders if people (himself included) are really willing to do whatever it takes to live as Christ would; in thought, deed, and action. He challenges himself, and whoever wants to join him, to commit to not doing *anything* for a full year without first asking the question: What would Jesus do in this situation?

The "What Would Jesus Do" (WWJD) phenomenon that sprouted up as a result of this writing was remarkable. A grassroots movement began in the 1990s and WWJD could be found on bracelets, bumper stickers, t-shirts, temporary tattoos, and on anything else motivated Christians

> For God did not send the Son into the world to judge the world, but that the world might be saved through Him.
>
> John 3:17

Why people leave a church:

✝ 10% Go to be with the Lord

✝ 12% Go to a job relocation

✝ 12% Prefer another church

✝ 66% Go because they are offended

WHEN A BELIEVER USES HIS WORDS TO BRING CONDEMNATION INSTEAD OF BRINGING LIFE PEOPLE WILL BE DRIVEN AWAY FROM CHURCH

could think to write it on.

Asking yourself WWJD before making a decision is a solid strategy for good decision making. The problem is, over time, Christians began to use it as a statement of judgement or condemnation against each other. Instead of asking oneself, "WWJD in this situation?" People began taunting each other when they saw someone doing something they shouldn't be.

You can almost hear the bitter admonition, "Jesus wouldn't do that! You better ask yourself WWJD!" declared from one disappointed Christian to another.

WWJD was so popular, even non-believers began to use it against Christians when they spotted a modicum of action that they viewed as hypocrisy.

This book and my evangelistic ministry **What Jesus Did** is abbreviated WJD. The reason I stand behind WJD is because a person cannot possibly understand how Jesus would act in a situation until they understand What Jesus Did for them in terms of their salvation story. We cannot condemn one another with haughtiness and judgement: "What Would Jesus Do?" Instead, I believe we should be asking people, "Do you understand **What Jesus Did** for you?"

In this week's study, I will better explain to you what exactly it was that Jesus did for you. As you understand the depth to which Jesus went for YOU, I believe you will be strengthening your confidence in how to share WJD for each and every person you encounter.

Week 2: What Jesus Did

DAY ONE - JESUS GIVES LIFE

ANDREAS' STORY

In 1996 I had the opportunity to minister at the Summer Olympics in Atlanta, Georgia. On my way to an event, the van I was driving got a flat tire. As I began to change the tire, I realized the factory lug wrench didn't fit the lug nuts.

I trotted back a half a mile to a convenience store for help. I picked a guy out of all the people in the store and asked what kind of car he drove. It was the same brand as mine AND he had a 4-way wrench in his trunk.

"I'm trying to get to the Olympic Village," the guy said. "I have to drive that way, so I can take you back to your car."

"Praise God!" I thought.

He drove me back to the van. Just as we were about to begin to change the tire, another man in a little truck pulled up and hopped out.

"Hey man, I want to help you," he said with excitement. He pulled out a shop floor jack from the back of his truck. "I don't want any money, I just want to help."

He began to work on my tire, leaving me with the opportunity to talk to the man from the convenience store. It dawned on me to ask him why he was going to the Olympic Village.

"I'm a track and field athlete from Russia," he explained. "My wife is, too, and she is waiting for me there."

"That's amazing!" I said. "I'm here to minister to athletes. Do you have a minute to talk?"

There on the side of a busy interstate, with cars whizzing by and the temperature up at 95 degrees, I talked to him about Jesus. I related it to striving for a medal in the Olympics. I told him that here on earth we try and win medals of gold, silver, or bronze. Eventually those medals and our earthly accomplishments will fade away. I told him that Jesus had a prize for us that will never perish. The gift of eternal life. Jesus's death and resurrection made the way for each person to reign in heaven as a champion when we die, and right now, on earth, Jesus's followers have a helper to work with us through our challenges and to guide us. I then asked him outright if there was any reason he had for not accepting Jesus's gift of salvation right then and there.

"No," he said.

"Would you like to pray to accept Christ right now as your Lord and Savior?"

"Yes," he declared. And right there, while a God-sent helper changed my tire, Andreas and I prayed. Andreas asked Jesus to be Lord of his life.

As Andreas was getting back into his car, and I was walking back to mine, I heard a yell from behind me.

"Hey!" he said.

"What?" I called back, turning around.

Andreas pounded his chest with his fists. "Andreas feels stronger!" he yelled in his thick Russian accent.

1. Andreas declared that he felt stronger after he accepted Jesus. Did you feel a change inside when you accepted Christ? Do you feel differently after you have been in deep prayer or after studying God's word?

Take My yoke upon you and learn from Me, for I am gentle and humble in heart, and YOU WILL FIND REST FOR YOUR SOULS. For My yoke is easy and My burden is light.
           Matthew 11:29-30

Sometimes we do feel a physical strengthening in our connection to Christ. This is because one of the things Jesus did for us is to remove the burden of our sins. He has lifted the weight of eternal damnation from us. Depending how old you were when you accepted Christ, you might have been carrying years of bad choices, regrets, hard feelings, and sadness. Jesus lifted those from you. You are free from their weight.

When someone comes to Christ for the first time and realizes that weight is gone, they might feel physically better. One man said to me once, after receiving Christ, "Wow! I feel lighter!"

Week 2: What Jesus Did

Read the passage below from Ezekiel 37:1-14.

The hand of the Lord was upon me, and He brought me out by the Spirit of the Lord and set me down in the middle of the valley; and it was full of bones. 2 He caused me to pass among them round about, and behold, there were very many on the surface of the valley; and lo, they were very dry. 3 He said to me, "Son of man, can these bones live?" And I answered, "O Lord God, You know." 4 Again He said to me, "Prophesy over these bones and say to them, 'O dry bones, hear the word of the Lord.' 5 Thus says the Lord God to these bones, 'Behold, I will cause breath to enter you that you may come to life. 6 I will put sinews on you, make flesh grow back on you, cover you with skin and put breath in you that you may come alive; and you will know that I am the Lord.'"

7 So I prophesied as I was commanded; and as I prophesied, there was a noise, and behold, a rattling; and the bones came together, bone to its bone. 8 And I looked, and behold, sinews were on them, and flesh grew and skin covered them; but there was no breath in them. 9 Then He said to me, "Prophesy to the breath, prophesy, son of man, and say to the breath, 'Thus says the Lord God, "Come from the four winds, O breath, and breathe on these slain, that they come to life."'" 10 So I prophesied as He commanded me, and the breath came into them, and they came to life and stood on their feet, an exceedingly great army.

11 Then He said to me, "Son of man, these bones are the whole house of Israel; behold, they say, 'Our bones are dried up and our hope has perished. We are completely cut off.' 12 Therefore prophesy and say to them, 'Thus says the Lord God, "Behold, I will open your graves and cause you to come up out of your graves, My people; and I will bring you into the land of Israel. 13 Then you will know that I am the Lord, when I have opened your graves and caused you to come up out of your graves, My people. 14 I will put My Spirit within you and you will come to life, and I will place you on your own land. Then you will know that I, the Lord, have spoken and done it,"' declares the Lord.'

2. How are the bones described when Ezekiel first saw them?

3. What kind of quantity of bones were there?

4. What did God tell Ezekiel to do to the bones?

5. Highlight or circle every use of the word "life" or "alive."

6. What made the bones come alive?

When you tell someone that God has a place for them in His kingdom <u>and</u> a plan for their life right now, you begin to speak the words that can bring LIFE to a spiritually dry soul.

EZEKIEL SPOKE GOD'S WORD AND HE TOLD THEM THAT GOD HAD A PLAN FOR THEM

You must remember that the people you are evangelizing to are like those bones. They are scattered, they are very dry, and there are very many of them. Their spiritual condition is like those of the bones; dry, dead, and chaotic. Verse 11 says that they have no hope. BUT! When Ezekiel speaks the word of God over those dry bones, things begin to happen!

They respond to the word of God first by making noise. The chaos begins to have order. The bones gain joints and muscles, which bring ability and strength. Then they are covered with a protection of skin. Finally, God provides breath, His Spirit, and they come to LIFE!

Ezekiel's prophesy includes both speaking God's word AND telling the bones what God will do for them. He declared that God had a place picked out for them, and that God had a plan for them.

As you evangelize, you must be prepared to tell people, who are as dry as those bones, that what Jesus did gives them access to God. And God has a good plan for their life. He has a place and purpose. He gives strength and ability. Most importantly, a relationship with Jesus will give LIFE!

Week 2: What Jesus Did

DAY TWO - JESUS GIVES PASSION

1. Think back to the last person who hurt you or offended you in some way. What was the circumstance and how did you feel about that person afterward?

According to the National Center for Charitable Statistics, there are more than 1.5 million non-profit organizations in the United States. Many of those are causes committed to helping people better some aspect of their lives. No matter how passionate the founders and supporters of those charities are, no one has ever demonstrated a passion for the state of mankind like Jesus did. No matter how hard to we try, on our own strength we can never show or exemplify passion in the way Christ did. We just don't have it in us.

Jesus tells us we are to love one another, but let's face it, at times it is downright impossible. There are people we simply do not want to show Jesus's love to. There are people we just don't have "Jesus-like" passion for. I'd go as far to say that the majority of Christians don't even feel the passion for Jesus that they should.

In your frustration of trying to live this Christian life, you will finally come to the understanding that the only possible way to show humanity your passion for

Jesus is to be living with Christ as leader over your life. Even when you have accepted Christ, your humanness will get in your way.

You must understand that Jesus was not only human, but He was also God incarnate. Jesus was able to see people in a way that we are not able to, because He was the one who created them. When Jesus showed love to humanity, He did so because His love, His passion, is beyond our finite mind. He loves differently.

Most people will have a hard time understanding this, but let me try and put this into a perspective you can understand.

If you knew someone was going to kill you, would you want to do *anything* nice for that person? Of course you wouldn't. That is where we must look at the love and passion Jesus has for us.

Picture Jesus, just a few hours away from being arrested in the Garden of Gethsemane. In the garden, He prayed to His Father. He knew the time of His death was at hand and He felt the pressure of what was about to happen. Scripture explains that while Jesus was praying, He was sweating large drops of blood.

As we consider Jesus's passion, you and I both need to understand that Jesus underwent cruel torture. Here's the thing. YOU had a personal involvement in every beating, every lash, every soldier's taunt, every thorn that dug into His head, every pound of the nail into His hands, every bit of pain He felt. YOU.

You weren't alone. I was part of it, too. So was your pastor, your BFF, your spouse, and your kids.

All of humanity had a part in murdering the Messiah.

And being in agony, He was praying very fervently; and His sweat became like drops of blood, falling down upon the ground.

Luke 22:44

JESUS WAS IN AGONY KNOWING WHAT WAS TO COME. HE KNEW HIS BEATING AND DEATH WOULD BE HORRIFIC, BUT HE ENDURED IT ANYWAY. FOR YOU.

But many were amazed when they saw him. His face was so disfigured he seemed hardly human, and from his appearance, one would scarcely know he was a man.

Isaiah 52:14

Week 2: What Jesus Did

2. Did you ever think of yourself as a murderer? How does the thought that you played a part in the torture and subsequent death of Jesus make you feel inside?

3. I had you list a person in question #1 who offended or hurt you. Since you are reading this study, I can assume that the person you named did not murder you. Know this: Jesus never felt that way about you, even though He died for your sin. He did it because He loved you then, and He loves you now. Knowing He has enough passion to die for you, visit hell for you, rise for you, and give you eternal life, how do you think you should feel for Him?

4. Considering what you wrote about how you should feel about Jesus, how do you think Jesus wants you to feel about the person you named in question #1. Does thinking about Jesus's passion for you give your passion for others a boost?

When evangelizing, if you find yourself losing passion for telling others what Jesus did, I urge you to go back to the story of His death on the cross. Jesus died with a passion for you. Draw from His passion as you go out and make disciples. He created the person you evangelize to, and He loves them far more than you ever will. Cling to His passion.

DAY THREE - JESUS GIVES HEALING
DONNA'S STORY

Donna was diagnosed with cancer when she was 30 years old. It began with an abdominal tumor that spread throughout her body and then into her brain. The doctors tried various aggressive treatments, but to no avail. Her body became destroyed and she was given a terminal prognosis. Donna had never been married; in her view, she'd never found the "right guy." But throughout all of her adult years, she had a friend named Howard. Howard had always loved Donna, even though she never saw him as a romantic interest. However, as she fought through her cancer, Howard remained by her side. In her sickness, she saw his love for her. When Howard asked her, "Donna, would you marry me before you die?" her answer was a resounding, "Yes!"

They didn't have much time. We rallied our community to help make the wedding beautiful. Florists donated more flowers than I could even describe to you. People Howard didn't know, found out about the service and showed up with some of the best food in town. Someone provided a wedding dress for Donna to wear.

Friends planned a renaissance-themed wedding. My sister Nylene, who works with horses, provided a horse for her to ride in on. My brother Johnnie dressed as a court jester, and led the horse in. Howard waited at the outdoor altar, dressed as a knight.

Howard stayed by his bride's bedside throughout the remainder of her sickness. On the day Donna died, Howard described her last moments to me as follows:

"Donna was in a type of coma that rendered her unresponsive. She was unable to talk, she wasn't showing any emotions, and had no movement. She was lying in her bed and I was sitting next to the bed, leaning against her. I felt a movement in the bed. I looked at her. Her eyes were open and she was sitting up. She wasn't looking at me. Her eyes were focused upward, smiling at something I couldn't see. She reached, as if she were taking ahold of someone's hand. Her face glowed and showed no sign of pain. She had no sign of sickness. There was a strength and a radiance that I'd never seen. Then she laid back on her bed and took her last breath."

At her funeral service, I shared that Howard witnessed a miracle. He got to see the woman he loved transform from her sick, physical human body into her pure, whole, healed, eternal glory.

Jesus's very name means salvation, deliverance, and to gain victory.

When evangelizing, remember this: the person who doesn't know Jesus has a terminal sickness. That sickness is eternal damnation of their soul. I have used this analogy before in my evangelism discussions: Let's say you came to me and you tell me that you have cancer. I have the cure for your cancer. I can make you well. But instead of sharing the solution with you, instead, I say to you, "I'm sorry to hear you're going to die," and I turn and walk away, with the cure in my pocket, never giving it to you.

What kind of monster would that make me?

When a non-believer stands before you, and you see their spiritual pain, you hear words of frustration, you sense their disappointment with life–and you do nothing about it–are you withholding the very thing that can cure their pain?

> The Hebrew word 'yasha' means to be open, to be wide or free, help, preserve, rescue, defend, deliver, be safe, bring salvation, save, and get victory.
>
> Jesus's Hebrew name 'Yeshua' is derived from this word, but with two additions. Yeshua also includes in its meaning 'health' and 'prosperity.'

1. When we accept Christ, we are saved from the terminal prognosis of eternal damnation. However, until He calls us to heaven, we will still experience both physical sickness here on earth, and the pain caused by the spiritual battles we must face every day.

Who is God laying on your heart right now, as someone who needs either the eternal cure, the initial saving healing that Jesus brings, or needs a healing word from Scripture to help them in their current struggle?

Journaling

In 1989 I lost a friend who I never took the opportunity to share the gospel to. It hit me pretty hard. Since then, I've shared this poem with thousands upon thousands of people over the past 20+ years.

I felt a heavy burden on my heart. Following my friend's death, I realized that because I call myself a believer in Jesus, I have a responsibility to tell everyone, whether they are my friend or not, what Jesus did for them.

Do you have a regret in your own life from a time when you didn't take hold of the chance to tell someone about Jesus, and then lost that opportunity forever?

How did you feel?

I'm not asking you this question to heap guilt on you. I want you to take that frustration, regret, whatever you feel, and heap it onto those who are still alive today. Concentrate your energy now on those who still have a chance.

My Friend

My friend I stand in judgement now,
And feel that you're to blame somehow.
On earth I walked with you by day,
And never did you point the way.

You knew the Lord in truth and glory,
But never did you tell the story.
My knowledge then was very dim,
You could have led me safe to Him.

Though we lived together here on earth,
You never told me of the second birth.
And now I stand this day condemned,
Because you failed to mention Him.

You taught me many things, that's true,
I called you "friend," and trusted you.
But I learn now that it's too late,
And you could have kept me from this fate.

We walked by day, and talked by night,
And yet you showed me not the light.
You let me live, and love, and die,
You knew I'd never live on high.

Yes, I called you "friend" in life,
And trusted you through joy and strife.
And yet, on coming to this dreadful end,
I cannot, now, call you, "my friend."

Love Someone in Christ.

~ David Soesbee

Week 2: What Jesus Did

When we are sick, we want to be healed. Those who don't know Jesus have the terminal sickness I spoke of earlier. After salvation, though, we will still experience things we need Jesus to bring healing to in our lives. Some places we need healing include: physical problems, health matters, relationships, emotional battles, finances, anxieties, addictions, unhealthy compulsions, obsessions, pursuit of sin.

We must bring all of these to Jehovah-Rapha, The Lord Who Heals.

> In the Bible, God is called by many names. Each name is used very intentionally, for the purpose of giving you depth and insight into God's character. Each name is a promise that you can count on. One of God's names is Jehovah-Rapha, which means: The Lord Who Heals.

2. In your Bible, look up the following verses. In the space below write down what Jehovah-Rapha, The Lord Who Heals, promises or declares in the verse.

Exodus 15:26

Jeremiah 30:17

Jeremiah 3:22

Isaiah 61:1

Psalm 103:3

The person you are evangelizing to needs healing. He or she may think their primary healing need relates to one of the things I listed (health, emotions, relationships, etc.), but if the spiritual healing never happens, the rest of it is all moot. You must guide them into that realization that God promises help in the other areas, but first He wants to make sure the terminal, eternal sickness is cured.

DAY FOUR - JESUS GIVES LOVE

I love my wife. I know without a doubt that she is one of the most beautiful women on this earth. I love her so much, I would fight for her. I would do absolutely anything and everything to protect her. My heart bursts with love for her when we are together and I miss her touch when we are apart. And I know she adores and loves me in return. But as much as I love her, and as much as she loves me, on the day that we die, our love for each other will not get us into heaven.

Your love for what Jesus did for you is the thing that breaks down the barrier between you and God. Some people will never love Jesus. They will reject Him and, as such, will spend eternity apart from Him.

I frequently run across Christian men and women who have an appreciation of what Jesus did for them, but never reach the depth of love for Him that He has for us. They love their spouses, their kids, even some hobbies and sports teams more than they love Jesus.

The things, big and small, that my wife does for me build into my love for her. If my wife was in a life-threatening situation, and I could take her place, I would die for her. But even that is not at the depth of what Jesus did for me. Jesus didn't only die for me, he went to hell for me. Then He arose and defeated death for me. That is something no one else can ever or will ever do. It is something no one else has ever done.

Most people have never fallen in love with Christ. The deeper you understand how much Christ loved you, the more you will be unable to stop telling people about Jesus. That is my prayer for you as you begin this last lesson for the week.

Week 2: What Jesus Did

1. On a scale of 1 - 10 with 1 being "no love at all" and 10 being "madly, passionately, couldn't possibly love any more" where would you rank your love for your spouse?
(If you aren't married, then rank the person closest to you: parent, sibling, kids, BFF)

1   2   3   4   5   6   7   8   9   10

Using the same criteria, rank your love for Jesus:

1   2   3   4   5   6   7   8   9   10

Using the same criteria, what do you think Jesus would mark if He was asked that question about you?

1   2   3   4   5   6   7   8   9   10

My wife and I both answered 10 for each other. If I had selected 10 and she selected 3 I'd say we had a bit of a relationship problem, wouldn't you? But when you look at your love for Jesus compared to His love for you, how far off were you from a 10 for Jesus?

Now, maybe you answered a 10 for your love for Jesus because you really do love Him that much. Let me ask you, and answer honestly, if someone else were to look at how you live your life, would they say you love Jesus at a 10 level?

For purposes of getting you thinking about your love for Jesus, I used a 1 to 10 ranking for His love for you, but in reality, His love for us is not even something we could chart. He loves you so far beyond a 10 it's unfathomable. And His love for us is a completely different type of love than the love we feel inside when we describe love.

IF SOMEONE ELSE WERE TO LOOK AT HOW YOU LIVE YOUR LIFE, HOW MUCH WOULD THEY SAY THAT YOU LOVED JESUS?

> He who has My commandments and keeps them is the one who loves Me; and he who loves Me will be loved by my Father, and I will love him and will disclose Myself to him. Judas (not Iscariot) said to Him, "Lord, what then has happened that You are going to disclose Yourself to us and not to the world?"
> Jesus answered and said to him, "If anyone loves Me, he will keep My word; and My Father will love him, and We will come to him and make Our abode with him."
>
> John 14:21-23

> When the Helper comes, whom I will send to you from the Father, that is the Spirit of truth who proceeds from the Father, He will testify about Me, and you will testify also, because you have been with Me from the beginning.
>
> John 15-26-27

Most often, we love one another with love that is translated from the Greek words "eros," "philia," or "storge."

- Eros love is a romantic love. It is love that comes with desire and longing. It is emotional and intimate love.
- Philia love is a brotherly, affectionate kind of love. It is the 'give and take' kind of love we often have for our friends.
- Storge love is a familial love. It is more affectionate in nature than passionate, and is used to refer to love for family.

When we think of love we often are referring to one of those three kinds of love. Christ's love is radically different. The Greek word used to describe God's and Jesus's love is agape. Agape love is a love that puts the needs of the person being loved ahead of the one doing the loving. Eros, philia, and storge love all have a selfish element to them. There is something the one doing the loving gets from the equation. But agape love is all about the person being loved. The one doing the agape is more concerned for the other person's well-being than he is for his own.

That is the love Jesus had for His Father, and for us. It is the love that compelled Him to the cross to die for you.

We cannot manufacture agape love on our own. We only get it from Jesus Himself. In John chapters 14 and 15 Jesus explains that those who love Him will obey Him. When we love Jesus, He sends His Holy Spirit to come to us. This is critical because as you can see from the verses I listed on the left, we need the Holy Spirit in order to testify about Christ.

Week 2: What Jesus Did

How does love translate while evangelizing? Many people would say that evangelizing is one person being pushy to another as they try and convince them to believe what they believe. Those who don't get it call evangelists "intolerant" or "unloving." Nothing is further from the truth.

If you saw a person give another person a huge, linebacker-style shove that sent them flying to the ground, you'd probably think that pushing someone violently over is a pretty unloving thing to do.

But what if what you didn't see is that the person who got shoved was someone who was both blind and deaf, and they were standing in the middle of a street with a semi-truck barreling toward them. The person who pushed them did so in order to get them safely out of the way quickly, saving their life. In context of the bigger picture, the act of shoving was a pretty loving, risky thing to do, wasn't it?

So it is with evangelizing. You are the one who sees the person standing in the middle of a street. But you see the bigger picture. You know the person in the road is blind and deaf to the danger around them. You see the truck. You know what will happen if you don't do something to get that person to safety. You have a moral obligation to do something. If you love Jesus, you will do what He commands. You will allow His Holy Spirit to speak through you and testify about what Jesus did for that person. The Holy Spirit is waiting to testify. It's one of His duties. You have to be open and willing to let it happen. Remember, as Jesus taught, those who love Him will do as He commands. (John 14:21, John 15:10, John 15:14)

Questions for Group Discussion:

Always begin your small group time with prayer.

1. In this week's study, we looked at 4 of the things that Jesus did for you. Jesus gives LIFE, Jesus gives PASSION, Jesus gives HEALING, and Jesus gives LOVE. Of these four (life, passion, healing, love), which is the easiest for you to talk about with someone, especially someone who is a non-believer? Why?

2. Which is the most difficult? Why?

3. For the thing that is most difficult for you to talk about with a non-believer, what is something you can do to become more comfortable discussing that aspect of Jesus?

4. On page 48, I suggested you journal about a time when you missed the chance to share your faith, and that opportunity got lost forever. In your small group, discuss your situations. Can you turn your regret into a fire and passion to see others come to accept Christ?

5. Do you ever think about the statement from Jesus that "those who love Him obey His commands"? Would someone else be able to look into your life and say you love Jesus?

WEEK THREE
REMOVING YOUR BARRIERS

THE STORY OF THE GREEKS ON THE BUS

While ministering in Athens during the 2004 Olympics, I wanted to try and see some of the Olympic soccer action. The soccer games were taking place at a location that was far south of Athens and would require me to take a subway train and several buses to get there. It was very confusing for me, and I had to keep stopping people and asking them to guide me to where I could catch my next bus. The bus numbering system made no sense to me, and the buses kept changing numbers, making it hard to understand if I was even getting onto the right bus. I finally got there and watched two games. When it was time for me to head back, it was late in the evening.

I seemed to be the only American at this game, and there were very few English-speaking people around. I found someone who directed me to an area where I could catch the bus. They told me what bus number to look for. Once on that first bus, I began asking people where I should get off, so I could be ready.

A large group of 25 to 30 young adults got on the bus. I started talking to them, showing them my map and address where I was trying to get. While talking, I realized no one understood what I was saying. After a couple of minutes of this, a girl from the back of the group pushed her way to me and asked, "Can I help you? I speak a little English."

As we talked, others from her group, began to ask her what I was saying. She would translate our conversation to the others as it went along. As they all looked at the map and I showed where I needed to be, she determined for me that I was on the right bus and it would be 50 minutes to an hour until my stop came up. But the group was on the bus even longer, so they would let me know when to get off.

Then she asked if I was in Athens to enjoy the Olympics. I explained that I was there for the Olympics, but not just to watch, I was there to minister to people and tell them about Jesus. She asked, "What do you mean by 'minister'?"

I began to tell her about what Jesus had done for me in my life. Remember, as I was talking, she kept pausing and translating my words for the others to hear. As I continued to speak, her friends in the group began asking questions that they wanted her to ask me. Many of them came from a Greek Orthodox background (the national religion of Greece). I shared my testimony with them, as I shared with you in the Introduction of this book. When I got to the part about God impressing on Dr. Johnson's heart to call me before I picked up the phone and called him, there was a murmur of an incredulous, "Ooooh," from them all. I picked up on that response and asked, "Have any of you ever asked God to reveal Himself to you?"

Instead of answering, someone from the group wanted me to continue with my story. I told them that through the experience, God showed me that He was real. I have to admit, my eyes teared and I began to cry. When I got to the part about Dr. Johnson explaining to me why Jesus loved me, I looked at them all and said, "Jesus loves each and every one of you. In fact, Jesus impressed on my heart to fly 7,000 miles from America for no other reason but to tell you that Jesus loves you."

They asked me to continue, and I did, all the way to the point where I prayed and received Christ. I told them that on that day, my life radically changed. I said that Jesus forgave me for the things I had done in my life that were sin. I asked them if they had ever had to forgive someone for something done against them. Many nodded. I said, "That's how it is with us and Christ. We've done something against Him. We have to ask Him to forgive us. And He will."

I often carry small buttons that read, "I am loved." I hand them out to people when I am traveling and tell them, "I'd like to give you a gift. When you see this button, let it remind you that there is a crazy American somewhere in the world who cares about you. But more importantly, let it remind you that Jesus loves you more than anyone ever has or ever will."

I handed out my buttons to the group. They smiled and said, "efxaristo" (thank you). I said to them, "Just as I gave you this gift, Jesus wants to give you His free gift. His gift will never fade or perish. I see you were excited to receive the gift I gave you,

Week 3: Removing Your Barriers

but would any of you like to receive the gift that Jesus has for you?"

The girl who was translating put her hand up. She said, "I would like to ask for this gift of Jesus." About eighteen others in the group also put their hands up and said they, too, wanted the free gift of Jesus.

There, on the bus, I prayed. She prayed after me, then translated the prayer for the others. The others would then say the prayer out loud in Greek. I was amazed. I made sure she told them it wasn't the words of the prayer that had the power, but it was the condition of their hearts that God saw.

When I got on that bus, I had a need. I needed to get back. When they got on the bus, they had a spiritual need they weren't aware of. God, in His infinite wisdom, knew all of our needs and He met them.

In this week's study, we will discuss the barriers you may be facing that you think keep you from being able to evangelize. My prayer is that you'll see that no matter what road blocks you feel you have–whether they are fear, language barriers, feelings of worthlessness, uncertainty of how to begin–whatever your reasons, God can meet your need from His endless power supply.

DAY ONE - "I'M AFRAID"

1. When you think about evangelism, do you have any fears? If so, list them below. What specifically are you afraid of when it comes to telling someone who doesn't believe in Jesus about your faith?

Fear definition

[noun] an unpleasant emotion caused by the belief that someone or something is dangerous, likely to cause pain, or a threat

[verb] be afraid of (someone or something) as likely to be dangerous, painful, or threatening

When it comes to fear and evangelism, here are the reasons people have given to me over the years for why they don't share their faith:

1. People will find out the rotten things I did before I knew Jesus and they'll think badly of me.
2. People will reject me or not like me anymore.
3. People become offended that I am trying to change their belief system.
4. I'll be seen as a religious, Jesus-freak.
5. I don't know how to begin.
6. I'll be asked a question that I won't know how to answer.
7. The other person will have another faith (Muslim, Buddhist, Jehovah's Witnesses) and I don't know anything about those faiths.

If you listed any of those concerns, you're in the right place. We're going to address them in the upcoming days of study. But today, I want you to see what God has to say about dealing with fear of any sort.

God decided what physiological changes our bodies would experience as a result of fear. Elevated heart rate, accelerated breathing, muscle tension, sweating, constricted blood vessels–these are some of the body changes that can happen when you are afraid. When we feel fear, we do something about it. We deal with the danger (or perceived danger) before us, or we get away from it. Fear is linked to survival.

Healthy fear is good for us, and can keep us safe. Unhealthy or unnecessary fears keep us from growing and pose a danger for those around us.

Week 3: Removing Your Barriers

We aren't going to do an in-depth study of healthy vs. unhealthy fear. I am going to state clearly: being afraid to evangelize and share your faith is an unhealthy fear and I'm going to give you biblical evidence to back that up.

2. Look up the following verses in your Bible. What are the key instructions God gives or information He provides us about fear?

Psalm 56:11

2 Timothy 1:7

1 John 4:18

Isaiah 41:10

Joshua 1:9

3. Return to Acts 9:1-22 (found on pages 31-32 of this study) and reread verses 10-17. What did God tell Ananias to do?

4. Did Ananias know who God was telling him to evangelize to?

5. How did Ananias respond?

6. To clarify, how had Saul been treating Christians prior to his experience with Ananias? (see verses 1-2)

Crushing the Giant

FEAR is a giant, much like the Goliath that a young David faced in 1 Samuel 17. Goliath was over 9 feet tall. David was a small shepherd boy. No one in Israel had the backbone to face Goliath. But David didn't need anything except for God. David told Goliath, "You come against me with sword and spear and javelin, but I come against you in the name of the LORD Almighty" (v.45).
Guess what? David killed that giant with nothing but a small stone.

Whether your Goliath is FEAR or something else that you come up against, I want you to know this:

If God has placed a Goliath in front of you, then He has placed a David inside of you.

If ever there was someone who should have been afraid to evangelize to someone else, it would have been Ananias. The guy God was sending him to had been killing his brothers and sisters in Christ. And Ananias knew it! Yet, he got up, and did as God said. He shared the truth about Jesus with Saul, and Saul became the rockstar of evangelists. He was used to write parts of the Bible, and the story of his life and conversion continues to lead people to Christ today.

Frequently in the Bible, when God calls someone to do something that might seem scary, He precedes His instruction with the words, "Do not be afraid. I am with you."

Jesus said, "These things I have spoken to you, so that in Me you may have peace." (John 16:33)

Peace is the opposite of fear.

When God sets the mission, He does not want us to approach it with fear. And God HAS set before us the task of telling others about Jesus. When we draw from Jesus's power source, we can be sure that He will supply what you need, when you need it, in order to accomplish the task. Therefore, we can have peace.

So let me ask again: What are you afraid of? If you can't trust the guy who just saved you from hell, who can you trust? Face your fear with faith. Face your fear with Jesus.

> **IF GOD HAS PLACED A GOLIATH IN FRONT OF YOU, THEN HE HAS PLACED A DAVID INSIDE OF YOU.**

Week 3: Removing Your Barriers

DAY TWO - "I DON'T WANT TO OFFEND"

There is a word that I think stifles more people from evangelizing than any other. That word is **tolerance**. Christians who know they should be sharing their faith often do not because they do not want to appear intolerant of other beliefs.

I'm going to tell you something: Tolerance is sending people to hell.

Non-Christians throw the word "tolerance" around because they do not want to feel the conviction inside when presented with the truth of Christ. In order for a person to repent and turn to Christ for salvation, they have to come to the realization that they have sinned against God. Some people fight coming to that conclusion. Not because they don't like you, but because Satan is fighting to keep their soul. The spiritual war is raging, and Satan will pull out all stops to keep someone from accepting Christ. Often, Satan's big trump card is to make the non-believer cry "intolerance!" at the Christian, who will promptly back down for fear of offending.

> If the world hates you, you know that it has hated Me before it hated you. If you were of the world, the world would love its own; but because you are not of the world, but I chose you out of the world, because of this the world hates you.
> John 15:18-19

> If I (Jesus) had not come and spoken to them, they would not have sin, but now they have no excuse for their sin.
> John 15:22

1. Read the two sets of verses listed on this page from John 15. In both passages, Jesus is speaking. Basically, Jesus is saying, "It isn't your fault they don't like the message. It is because you and they are operating from two totally different worlds." Jesus also tells us that once they know the truth, they are responsible for dealing with it. There's no excuse to continue in sin. Do Jesus's words in these verses give you any comfort when it comes to being afraid of offending someone with the message of Christ?

2. Have you ever had someone tell you that you were intolerant because of your Christian belief? Or have you heard it said that Christians were intolerant? How did you respond?

TOLERANCE DOESN'T MEAN YOU ROLL OVER AND ALLOW SOMEONE ELSE TO WALK ALL OVER YOUR FAITH.

It is a faulty belief that being tolerant means you have to accept the other person's belief as possibly true. Yes, someone is entitled to believe in evolution, other gods, or no god at all. But they are wrong. And if you think that in order to be respectful of their right to be wrong, that you should not ever present your faith or engage them in discussing Jesus, then you are wrong, too.

If someone told me, "You should be more tolerant of other faiths," here is how I would respond.

First I would ask them to give me their definition of tolerance. I would ensure their definition is accurate. I would say, "You have every right to your own opinion on matters of faith, of your own belief system, or your moral code."

But then I would tell them I would be happy to listen to whatever they say, as long as they are willing to give me the same respect and timeframe that I give them. Tolerance is not about me bending over backwards and letting someone walk all over me. It is me allowing the other person to express their opinion, whether I agree or disagree with them. To be tolerant does not mean "to be quiet."

Week 3: Removing Your Barriers

3. Read these verses from 1 Peter 3:13-16:

> Who is there to harm you if you prove zealous for what is good? But even if you should suffer for the sake of righteousness, you are blessed. And do not fear their intimidation, and do not be troubled, but sanctify Christ as Lord in your hearts, always being ready to make a defense to everyone who asks you to give an account for the hope that is in you, yet with gentleness and reverence; and keep a good conscience so that in the thing in which you are slandered, those who revile your good behavior in Christ will be put to shame.

According to these verses, how are we to explain the reason for our faith to others? What is our demeanor to be?

Notice Peter doesn't tell us, "Share about Christ with anger, argument, and fists a blazin'." He clearly states we are to speak with gentleness and reverence and with a good conscience. If you enter into an evangelistic moment ready for an argument, you will find the other person more than ready to fight back. This will be contrary to Christ's goal. However, not arguing doesn't mean rolling over and conceding defeat. It means speaking in a voice laced with love (agape) for the one you are speaking to.

4. Have you ever seen someone try to evangelize and it failed miserably?

5. Based on the verses we've studied so far on how we are to act as we share what Jesus did, why do you think the effort failed?

Evangelism isn't about arguing or getting into a fight about who is right and who is wrong. It is about presenting a different way. <u>The</u> way. <u>The</u> truth. <u>The</u> life. Christ does not need anyone to fight his battles. He already fought the battle. He won. He needs a willing vessel to tell people what he did. Just like He asked the 12 disciples to do.

The fact of the matter is, some people WILL be offended by the message of the cross. You can't help that or stop that. All you can do is be there to keep pointing the way to Jesus.

DAY THREE - "I'M NOT WORTHY"

1. Have you ever been around someone that you know does not like you? How do you know that person did not like you?

When we don't like someone, our general instinct is to avoid them. We don't call them. If it is a coworker, we take care to interact as little as possible. If it is a family member, we don't get into discussions with them. If it is someone who was a friend, but we've had a falling out, then we do what we can to remove them from our immediate circle.

I'd like to tell you that there is someone who hates you. He hates you with a burning, intense, ugly hate. And although if you ever felt a strong hate for someone you would remove them from your life, this guy does just the opposite. He plots out ways to

Week 3: Removing Your Barriers

destroy you. He makes plans to wreck your world and then will set wheels in motion to carry out those plans. Every day, he tries to convince you that lies are truth and that truth are lies.

I'm talking about Satan.

2. Look up each of the following verses. What do they reveal about Satan?

John 10:10

1 Peter 5:8

2 Corinthians 11:14

James 4:7

John 8:44

Look at those words you've written. THAT is what you're up against. As you go out to make disciples, you are trying to help move people from Satan's clutches into the palm of God's hand. Satan does not want that to happen. One way Satan tries to stifle potential evangelists is to convince them that they are not worthy of that task. He will remind you of your past. He will cause strife in your present. He will do whatever he can to prevent you from sharing what Jesus did for you.

If being reminded of your past is one of the tricks Satan uses against you, today I pray you will realize that Satan is reminding you of your past to wreck the future for you and those you love.

3. What do the following verses tell you about how God sees you?

Psalm 139:13-16

2 Corinthians 12:9

2 Corinthians 5:17

John 10:27-30

4. Who do you belong to?

5. Re-read John 8:44. Who does the non-believer belong to?

Every person on earth either belongs to God the Father or belongs to the father of lies. There are only two options. Satan will try and convince you of your unworthiness, but Satan can never snatch you from the hand of God once you are there.

Satan will also try and convince the person you are talking to that he or she is not worth God's time or His love. I experienced that firsthand. So did Gayla.

6. Go back to page 5 and page 21 of this study. In my story and in Gayla's story, we each had a moment of feeling unworthy of God's grace. What do you learn from reading the response of the evangelist who was ministering to each of us at the time?

I often hear people joking around about hell. It sounds absurd, but non-believers, especially those who are into the party scene, do it all the time. I know, because I was in that lifestyle. Those who die without Christ will not be sent to a party where booze, drugs, and rock-n-roll are overflowing in abundance. Satan isn't waiting for "his" people to arrive so the party can begin. Read the verses to the right. Does that sound like a party waiting to happen? It sounds like excruciating torment to me. Those in hell have no buddies.

That, my friend, is what is on the line. Satan isn't the unbeliever's friend. He hates everyone.

> But the cowardly, the unbelieving, the vile, the murderers, the sexually immoral, those who practice magic arts, the idolaters and all liars—they will be consigned to the fiery lake of burning sulfur. This is the second death.
> Revelation 21:8

> And the smoke of their torment goes up forever and ever; and they have no rest day and night.
> Revelation 14:11

DAY FOUR - "I DON'T KNOW HOW TO BEGIN"

Another barrier to evangelizing I frequently encounter is that people say, "I don't know how to begin the conversation." Long before you can begin an evangelistic conversation, there are some very important steps you need to follow. We learned in the previous lesson that you are up against Satan, the father of lies, in a spiritual battle with eternity on the line. How do you begin? You suit up.

1. What did the Jewish priests attempt to do? (v. 13)

2. Were they successful?

3. What happened to them? (v. 16)

4. Who was performing the miracles at Paul's hands? (v. 1)

5. Do you think God was involved when the Jewish priests tried to perform the same miracle that Paul had been performing?

    I think it is fair to say that the Jewish priests were attempting to operate under Jesus's name without true access to Jesus's power. The fact that Luke (who wrote Acts) described them as "Jewish priests" and not "believers" or as "disciples of Christ" is one indication. Another is the fact that they had no power over the evil spirit. If you try and evangelize in Jesus's name, but are not connected to Jesus through the Holy Spirit, you simply cannot expect God to be willing to perform a miracle through you. He wants you to seek Him first.

    Preparation for evangelism must begin with prayer. If you're not willing to take the time to put on the whole armor of God at the beginning of each day, then you won't stand strong at the end.

Week 3: Removing Your Barriers

Questions for Group Discussion:

Always begin your small group time with prayer.

1. Just as God provided for the needs of myself and the Greeks on the bus, recall and discuss a time when God clearly provided for your needs in a unique way. Thank Him for His provision.

2. After working through the lesson on overcoming fear, do you feel less afraid to step out and share your faith? If yes, what made the difference? If not, what specifically are you afraid of? What does God say about that fear?

3. How would you respond if someone said to you, "I would never become a Christian, because Christians are so intolerant"?

4. Can you recall a time you turned combative when talking about Jesus with someone? In hindsight, how might you have handled things differently?

5. If you came face to face with an evil spirit, would the evil spirit identify you as someone connected to Jesus's power? Or would it laugh in your face and say, "I know Jesus, but who are you?"

WEEK FOUR
THE COMPETITION

The Ichthys

Christians today put the "Jesus fish" on their cars, bumper stickers, signs, etc. to show others they follow Jesus. It's actually called the ichthys; which is the Greek word for 'fish.'

1st and 2nd century persecuted Christians used the ichthys as a secret symbol to let one another know of their faith. When two Christians would meet in the road, one would drag his foot in the dirt to make an arc (the top of the fish) and the other would use his foot to complete the picture. Then they would know they could talk freely about Jesus.

In my years of ministry, I have shared the gospel of Jesus Christ with people from dozens of different faiths and belief systems. Evangelizing scares some people because they think they don't know enough about other religions and beliefs so that they can accurately present information about Jesus in light of those other beliefs. For example, how is the Jesus you serve different from the Jesus that the Jehovah's Witnesses believe in? Is Allah just another name for God?

You do not have to be a religious studies scholar in order to evangelize to people of other faiths, but I do strongly recommend that you know some of the basic tenets that other religions operate from. In this week's study I will lay the groundwork for you to have a basic understanding of those major differences.

One thing that transcends all other faith systems is the concept of grace. You've likely heard it said that Christians are saved by grace and grace alone. Do you understand what that means?

In the space below, write down your definition

of grace. (Don't look it up, write from your understanding as it is right now.)

GRACE MEANS ...

You'll find that as we look at other belief systems, grace is the one thing we have that they don't. It's a tough concept to grasp because we think we have to "do" something to earn our place in heaven. You must understand this, because it is so contrary to other faith systems: There is nothing you can do to earn God's favor. He offers it right now, today, as you are. God is reaching down toward the person who needs saving. He is offering salvation through Jesus. Right now! That's grace.

We can be saved because He loved us before there was anything worth loving in us. That's grace.

He wants to have a relationship with you because He loves you. That's grace.

You can have His eternal riches, and you don't deserve them. That's grace.

Grace is difficult for non-believers to understand because Jesus's followers sometimes act with anything BUT grace. You will hear (if you haven't already) that Christians claim to be saved by grace, but they have no idea how to give that grace to others. I can't dispute it. I've seen Christians act in the most ungraceful ways imaginable. I explain to people who think this way that saying you won't accept Jesus because Christians act badly is like

Grace

Greek word: xáris (charis) - favor, disposed to, inclined, favorable towards, leaning towards to share benefit - properly, grace.

xáris is preeminently used of the Lord's favor - freely extended to give Himself away to people (because He is "always leaning toward them").

saying you won't ask your professor a question because the other students in the class are stupid. Or saying you won't go to the doctor because other patients in his office are sick. **Jesus** gives the grace for salvation. Other Christians are nothing more than a work in progress, just like you.

Each lesson in this week's study will compare the basics of some of the more popular religions you may encounter.

This week's lesson structure will differ from the other weeks. I will provide you with a "cheat sheet" that includes the basics of the faith we are studying. I then want you to do two things for each of these faiths.

1. Do some additional research (internet, reading, library, talking to experts) and add to your arsenal of knowledge about that faith.

2. Find a trusted Christian friend (spouse, Bible study partner, etc.) and role play as you explain the differences between Christianity and the other faith. You don't have to give an academic presentation, but see if you can recall the basics comfortably without any props.

Week 4: The Competition

DAY ONE - MUSLIM FAITH

Who do they serve? Muslims serve one god and his name is Allah. We cannot know Allah personally, and human qualities (like fatherhood) cannot be attributed to him.

How did Islam begin? Before Islam came to be, people in the Saudi area worshipped Allah, and Allah had gods and goddesses who were under him. Judaism and Christianity were present in Saudi prior to Islam's emergence. In 610 A.D., a man named Muhammad was fasting and praying in a mountain cave. He said that while praying, he received a revelation from the angel Gabriel. Gabriel brought Muhammad instructions from Allah. To remember them, Gabriel made him recite the verses, because Muhammad was illiterate and couldn't write or read. He continued to have several of these private visits from the angel. He said Allah told him these revelations were to supersede the Christian Bible teachings. He also said Allah told him that he (Muhammad) was the one true and last prophet to bring Allah's final revelation to the world. Muhammad communicated these things verbally to his followers, and eventually (after Muhammad died) they were written down into what became known as the Qur'an (Koran).

Muhammad rallied a small following behind his Qur'an teachings. That following (which had political and social aspirations) grew into more than a billion followers today.

What about Jesus? Muslims believe Jesus to be one of Allah's prophets. They do not believe Him to be God's Son or the Savior for the world. They reject the crucifixion and resurrection. They say the term "Holy Spirit" refers to Allah himself or to a spirit that Allah sends to give life to man or to give revelation to prophets. They do believe Jesus was born of a virgin and performed miracles.

What happens after death? Allah will decide whether someone ends up in heaven or hell, based on his good and bad deeds on earth and adherence to the Qur'an teachings. Allah's favor is the determining factor. They believe righteous men will be provided sexual pleasure in heaven by maidens designed for that purpose. A Muslim will go straight to heaven if he dies while fighting for the cause of Islam.

What Jesus Did for the Muslim:
Muslims do not believe that God can be known personally. I've evangelized to many Muslims over the years, and one thing they marvel at is the thought of a personal relationship with God. One explanation that I've had success breaking through that barrier is when I've said, "You serve a god who says you must serve and die for him. I serve a God who says, 'I will serve and die for YOU.' The God that I serve loves you and He loves everyone." Speaking to them about God's love is a radically different concept because they are taught to fear Allah's wrath.

Muslims discredit parts of the Christian Bible that do not align with the Qur'an. I've had Muslims ask me how I can believe the Bible is all true. At that point, I usually say that the archaeological evidence to support the validity of the Bible cannot be ignored. Muslims ignore the fact that nations, customs, kings, cities have all been discovered by historians to align with how they are described in the Bible. There has been more archaeological evidence found that proves the accuracy of the Bible than any other book or writing in the world.

Muslims know they cannot throw out the whole Bible, so instead they say that anything that does not agree with what Allah revealed to Muhammad must be false or has been corrupted by the Christians. They pick and choose the parts that they need to help make the Qur'an work. For example, they say Jesus existed, but they say he was a prophet and not God's Son. I point out the mismatch in their logic. "You say God sent Jesus to be a prophet, but you say Jesus lied when He claimed to be God's Son? Why would God send a liar?"

The most important thing, in my experience in evangelizing to a Muslim, is to speak of God's love. Allah doesn't care for them individually. Through Jesus we have the chance to know God personally, and the chance to have a relationship with Him. God also desires to give us His help here on earth. We aren't on our own trying to please a God who doesn't care for us. Speak to these things and share what Jesus did for you personally. Remember, the Muslim doesn't believe they will know if they go to heaven or hell until they stand before Allah on Judgement Day. Tell them that they can know right then, at that moment, that God will welcome them into His kingdom when they die because of what Jesus did.

Week 4: The Competition

DAY TWO - HINDUISM

Do Hindus believe in God? Actually, Hindus believe in more than 3 million gods! These gods are manifestations of the one Supreme God called Brahman. They believe we are all a part of Brahman, but the majority of people are not even aware of this. Life is a journey to become one with Brahman.

When did Hinduism begin? The oldest writings about Hinduism are dated around 1000 B.C. There is no one founder attributed to Hinduism. There are three main types (or sects) of Hindu worship. They share certain beliefs, traditions, and gods, but each one has a different philosophy on how to achieve the ultimate goal of life: liberation from oneself and unity with Brahman. That's what life is all about for a Hindu.

How do Hindus worship? Hindus show devotion to whichever personal gods or goddesses they choose to worship. Hindus worship stone or wooden idols of their chosen gods / goddesses. They place these statues or pictures in temples and around their homes. Worship and devotion happens through meditation, chanting, yoga, and breathing exercises. Yoga poses are positions of worship to different Hindu gods.

Hindus believe in the concept of karma. Karma means that one's actions and intentions will affect their future. In other words, if you do good deeds, then good things will happen to you. If you do something bad, something bad will happen to you. Karma can be repaid either in this lifetime, or in your next lifetime.

Do Hindus believe in Jesus? They recognize Jesus as a teacher. Just like all of us, Jesus is one of God's children. His death has no atonement for our sins. We are each responsible for our own karma. They do not believe Jesus rose from the dead. There is no Holy Spirit as part of Hindu belief.

What happens after death? Hindus believe in reincarnation. We cycle through this world until we are finally released into the universe and absorbed into, or made one with, Brahman. Yoga, meditation, and good karma help move us along.

What Jesus did for the Hindu:

Once, when I was speaking at a church in North Carolina, one of the church's youth brought her friend, a girl from India whose family was Hindu, to talk to me. I asked the girl to explain her beliefs to me. She listed many of the things I shared with you on the previous page. When she got to the part about reincarnation, I began to ask her questions. I asked her, "When you come back in another life, do you remember the previous life? Or are you starting over?" She didn't have a solid answer for that. She didn't know. I also asked her what her "heaven" was like. She said that no one can know for sure what it will be like. They will just become one with Brahman. She couldn't even accurately explain what or who Brahman was.

I used those two points to speak to her. I said, "Wouldn't you rather know that when your time is up here on earth, you are going to die only once? It sounds like through reincarnation you could have to die dozens, hundreds, if not thousands of times before you reach heaven!"

She said that dying once did sound better than dying many times. I also asked her if she would like to know for a fact that God is on her side, rather than hope that her devotion, meditation, and her karma is enough to make her god happy. Again she said, yes she would like to have that certainty.

I told her what Jesus did for her. I explained that He died and took the punishment for her. Through Him, she can accept His gift of salvation and know without a doubt that she will be with Him in heaven when she dies. She can know what that will be like, because the Bible tells us. That girl prayed to receive Christ that day, much to the anger of her father. He even threw her out of the house for a time. But she was firm in her faith. She ended up going to a Christian college and continued to grow in the Lord.

Week 4: The Competition

DAY THREE - JEHOVAH'S WITNESSES

What do they believe about God? Jehovah's Witnesses (J.W.) call God "Jehovah." They do not believe in the Trinity. They believe Jesus to be the first thing Jehovah created.

When did J.W. begin? Jehovah's Witnesses started in 1879 by a man named Charles Taze Russell. Russell was raised as a Christian, turned agnostic at age 17, then got re-interested in the Bible when he heard it preached that Jesus would return one day. He was strongly influenced by the Adventist church at that time, but when the Adventists' predictions of Jesus's return fell through, he went off on his own. He began *The Watchtower Society*, and began producing literature that is still in existence today. *The Watchtower* promotes values that J.W. believe are important. J.W. have a strong interest in the "end" of times. Russell erroneously predicted Jesus's return in 1914 and then again in 1925. J.W. later claimed Jesus *did* return in 1914, but His return was invisible. He and the angels will come back again "soon" visibly to destroy non-Jehovah's Witnesses.

J.W. do not meet in churches, but in "Kingdom Halls." Active members are encouraged to distribute *Watchtower* literature and tracts door-to-door and to invite others to come to Kingdom Hall meetings. This activity is part of their good deeds.

Do they believe in Jesus? They believe Jesus was Michael the Archangel when He lived in heaven, but when Jehovah sent Him to earth, He became Jesus. They will say Jehovah created all things through Jesus, but they do not believe Jesus to be God. They believe He died on a stake (not a cross) and was resurrected as a spirit only. The Holy Spirit is a force of Jehovah's and is not God.

What about heaven? J.W. believe that salvation in heaven is reserved for only 144,000 anointed ones, and this number has already been reached. The "rest of them" will be allowed to earn everlasting life on earth. Everlasting life on earth will begin "soon," when the angels come back and destroy all the non-Jehovah's Witnesses. At that time, they will have to obey God perfectly here on earth for 1,000 years or they will be forever destroyed.

But don't they have a Bible? The J.W. use a translation of the Bible called The New World Translation (NWT). They are the only group to use this translation, because they are the ones who translated it. The early members of *The Watchtower Society* realized that many of their beliefs were different from what the King James Bible presented. So, rather than conform their faith to what God's word said, they got their own group to translate the Bible to read the way they wanted.

It can seem overwhelming to evangelize to someone who belongs to a group who claims on some level to be "biblically-based." You must remember though, that even the Satanists have a bible. The problem is, their bible is NOT our Bible. J.W. translated the original Hebrew and Greek Scriptures to match their beliefs. They did not translate them from a scholarly and objective standpoint. The credentials of the scholars who translated the King James, New American Standard, NIV, etc. are verifiable and academically credible. The credentials of the 5 people who translated the NWT are nonexistent. In other words, they have no credentials. If you do get into a Scripture discussion with a J.W., its best to use either the King James or New American Standard versions for your support. They lend the most credibility to these sources.

What Jesus did for the Jehovah's Witnesses:
J.W. believe that earning everlasting life is based on your works. Remember, they don't think they are going to heaven, just striving for everlasting life on earth. When explaining the real Jesus to a J.W., I like to speak of the vast difference between our views of who Jesus is, what He did, and what happens when we die. God said we cannot earn our place in eternity. Jesus made getting to heaven possible through His atoning sacrifice, which is available to all who call on Him for salvation.

Just as when I dispute the teachings of the Qur'an, I point to the historical accuracy of the Bible. Their bible simply doesn't have the credentials to hold up as authoritative. My Bible clearly states that Jesus was God. My Bible clearly states that no man knows

Week 4: The Competition

the time or hour of Jesus's return. And my Bible clearly states that Jesus's return will not be an invisible occurrence. Every eye will see Him and will know He is Lord when He returns. They pick and choose and contort the Scriptures to match the NWT.

J.W. will ask you things like, "Aren't you fed up with the hypocrisy of other Christian denominations?" They will tell you that they are Christian and they will show you *Watchtower* literature that quotes Scriptures that are found in your Bible, too. They will probably show you the verse where Jesus calls His followers to go out and "make disciples." It will seem a lot like your Bible translation. But don't be fooled. They claim to be Christian, but their Jesus is not the Son of God. He is merely a man who cannot save you from your sins. Without Jesus, without the cross, without the resurrection, there is no salvation.

If you pay close attention to these other religions, you'll see how the founders of these faiths were not able to adhere to the word of God. Therefore, they started preaching their own false teachings to tickle the ears of people around them. They preached things that would let them continue to live their own personal lifestyle preferences. They twist, rewrite, and completely ignore the parts of the Bible that don't fit their worldly views.

Adolph Hitler left a legacy of death, destruction, hate, and evil behind. However, one of the truest things attributed to his regime was this statement: "If you tell a big enough lie, and tell it frequently enough, it will be believed." The devil tells lies about Christ. People who are deceived spread those lies about Christ. We who know better are responsible to tell the truth.

What Jesus Did Bible Study ✦ David Soesbee

DAY FOUR - MORMONISM (LATTER-DAY SAINTS)

What do they believe about God? Mormons believe that God the Father was once a man, and he progressed to god-status. They believe that God has a physical body, and his main wife, called the Heavenly Mother, has a physical body too. They believe that the Father, Son, and Holy Spirit (Holy Ghost) are three separate gods. They believe God the Father has eternal wives through whom spirit children have been and continue to be born.

When was Mormonism started? Joseph Smith is the founder of Mormonism. He claimed to have been visited several times by an angel (called Moroni) who was sent from God to reveal ancient gold plates with inscriptions on them. He enlisted the help of a man named Oliver Cowdery to write down what he (Smith) translated from the plates. This became the *Book of Mormon*. Three men, other than Smith, initially claimed to have seen the gold plates. This boosted the start of the religious movement, but those men (including Cowdery) later discredited Joseph Smith and said they never actually saw them.

In 1830 the first edition of *The Book of Mormon* was published and Smith began to gain a following in New York. Following Smith's death, the headquarters were moved to Salt Lake City, Utah by Brigham Young (Smith's successor), where they remain today.

How does Jesus fit in? Mormons (The Church of Jesus-Christ of Latter-day Saints) will tell you that they are Christian. They even have "Jesus Christ" in their name, so they must be Christian, right? Wrong. Their Jesus is not the Jesus of the Bible. First, they reject the virgin birth of Jesus, claiming God the Father had sexual relations with the Heavenly Mother, and Jesus was born as a spirit-baby. Because God is the Father of all spirits, Jesus is the brother of Lucifer (Satan), because Lucifer was also a spirit-baby of God the Father's. They believe that Jesus was married when He was on earth. Mormons acknowledge Jesus's death on the cross, but do not believe it provides atonement for our sins. They say Jesus is a different God from God the Father.

Week 4: The Competition

What happens when we die? Mormons believe that unless you are a Mormon, a part of the "one true church," you will not have eternal life. They will speak of God's grace, but they believe that everyone will go to one of three separate "kingdoms" when they die, based on their works and faithfulness to the Mormon teachings and Mormon leadership. They believe some worthy members will achieve godhood in eternity.

One thing I find interesting, and I want you to remember, is that two of the largest cults in the world, Mormonism and Jehovah's Witnesses, were founded right here in America, more than 1,800 years after Jesus walked the earth. Satan has used Russell and Smith to blind millions of people to the truth of who Jesus is. You don't need to get in an argument with them, you simply need to tell the truth about Jesus. Speak of knowing Jesus personally. Acknowledge that you have extremely different views of God, Jesus, and the Holy Spirit. If they try and tell you that your faiths are similar, politely beg to differ. Your God is not their God. Your Jesus is not their Jesus.

Like all cults, Mormons have had to adjust their beliefs over the years to continue to convince non-Mormons to buy into their lies and become part of their godless faith. Any religion that has to evolve and shift their truths because their teachings are discredited, should be a red-flag for you that it is a cult. Our faith in Christianity can be further solidified by this fact: Jesus, as presented in the Bible, has never changed. The message is the same today as it was thousands of years ago.

When evangelizing to a Mormon or J.W., remember one of the main ways they show allegiance to their faith is through their works. Knocking on doors of people who aren't part of their "church," trying to convince non-members to come to meetings or Bible studies, all contribute to their good deeds.

More Christians are leaving the Christian church and converting to Mormonism than ever before in history. Why? Because Mormons are really nice people. They show such love and talk about strong, moral family values that people are deceived into thinking that "if they are such nice people, their faith must be on track." Please hear me when I say this: nice people will go to hell if they don't accept Jesus Christ as their Savior.

Questions for Group Discussion:

Always begin your small group time with prayer.

1. I hope that you took the time this week to do some additional research on each of the religions presented in the lessons. Share and compare what else you learned with the members of your group.

2. Nowhere in the Bible do we read that "nice people go to heaven." Yet, many people believe this very thing. They may not know what heaven looks like, or what it will be all about, but they believe that if they are "good enough," then they'll get there when they die. How would you respond if someone said to you, "I believe I'll go to heaven when I die because I am a good person"?

3. Have you ever had a discussion with someone of another faith about your beliefs compared to theirs? How did it go?

4. When evangelizing, you do not have to refute someone else's faith. Your job is to present the truth about Jesus. They have an incorrect or distorted view of Jesus. They may come at you with slick Scriptures that sound good on the surface, but you should bring the discussion to who Jesus claimed to be in the Bible. Tell what Jesus did for you. Discuss in your group your comfort level talking to someone of a different faith about what Jesus did.

WEEK FIVE
BECOMING DISCIPLES

Most people struggle with evangelism because they don't understand how to move a conversation along towards sharing what Jesus did for them. As such, they feel awkward and uncomfortable. Those feelings come across to the other person, making the Christian seem ill-equipped and uncertain about their beliefs.

If you are confident that you have a relationship with Christ, the person you are sharing with should feel that confidence. I'm not saying you have to know everything. Nobody knows everything. But if you are confident in your personal salvation, there should be no hesitation or uncertainty in your words.

There are numerous presentation models that walk a person through the steps of evangelism. I'm talking about models like Evangelism Explosion (E.E.), The Four Spiritual Laws, People Sharing Jesus, Serving God, and so on. Having a model is good, but instead of worrying about memorizing someone else's model, don't you think it would be best to first get to know the other person, and then share your own personal experience with Jesus? The

> He who gives an answer before he hears,
> It is folly and shame to him.
>
> Proverbs 18:13

framework I present is one that I believe works in nearly every situation because it involves meeting the person right where they are, and sharing your story. Your own testimony is the only model you need to rely on.

In this week's lesson, we will go through what I feel are key components for an evangelistic conversation to be successful: Listening, Responding appropriately, Telling your story, Giving a choice.

DAY ONE - QUICK TO HEAR, SLOW TO SPEAK

> This you know, my beloved brethren. But everyone must be quick to hear, slow to speak and slow to anger.
> James 1:19

Evangelism is about communicating. Unfortunately, all of us aren't born with great communication skills. Communication skills must be practiced, developed, and honed.

I don't care if you are in a business setting, chatting with a friend, having a conversation with your spouse, or making small talk with a stranger while waiting in line to get a hotdog at a baseball game, listening is the key to effective communication.

Because I want you to get better at communicating your faith, today's lesson is all about listening.

In any conversation, there are two people you should be listening to:

1. The person who is speaking.
2. The Holy Spirit.

As you listen to the speaker, the Holy Spirit can prompt and nudge you as to how you should respond. A good evangelist is also a good listener. It's tempting

Week 5: Becoming Disciples

to think that being an evangelist is all about talking. But every person is not at the same level of prior exposure to who Jesus is. And until you learn where they are, you can't meet them there.

That's why I don't rely on any one model for sharing the gospel. If you had to give someone directions how to get to your house, the first question you will likely ask is, "Where are you coming from?"

It's the same way in a conversation. You need to know where the other person is coming from before you can direct them anywhere. The God we serve is so big, so creative, and so exciting, we cannot begin to imagine the things that the other person has been through up until the point they are talking to you. So let them talk. Rather, *invite* them to talk.

1. How comfortable are you initiating a conversation, and then encouraging someone to expand on what they are saying?

2. Think of a time when you had a really great conversation with someone you just met. What about it made the conversation successful?

Most people want to talk about themselves. Let's face it, we are a very "me-centered" society. When you are trying to build a rapport with someone, avoid the temptation to jump in, cut them off, or interrupt what they are saying so you can get to your part. And, you need to be listening for those things that the other person will say that will give you

insight into:
1. What they believe
2. Where you might have common ground
3. What problems they may be facing
4. How they spend their time
5. Their prior experience with Jesus

It is the Holy Spirit that will illuminate to you the thing, the pain, the stumbling block in this person's life that has been keeping them from God.

3. In Acts 16, Paul and Silas went on a missionary journey. While traveling, they freed a slave-girl from the torment of an evil spirit. This act landed them in prison. That is the backdrop for the Scripture I'd like you to study:

23 When they had struck them with many blows, they threw them into prison, commanding the jailer to guard them securely; 24 and he, having received such a command, threw them into the inner prison and fastened their feet in the stocks.

25 But about midnight Paul and Silas were praying and singing hymns of praise to God, and the prisoners were listening to them; 26 and suddenly there came a great earthquake, so that the foundations of the prison house were shaken; and immediately all the doors were opened and everyone's chains were unfastened. 27 When the jailer awoke and saw the prison doors opened, he drew his sword and was about to kill himself, supposing that the prisoners had escaped. 28 But Paul cried out with a loud voice, saying, "Do not harm yourself, for we are all here!" 29 And he called for lights and rushed in, and trembling with fear he fell down before Paul and Silas, 30 and after he brought them out, he said, "Sirs, what must I do to be saved?"

3. Highlight what Paul and Silas were doing right before the earthquake came.

4. Because they stayed, instead of fleeing when the chains came off, what was the result for the jailer?

Week 5: Becoming Disciples

Paul gives us the best example of an evangelist in the Bible. He was not only willing to tell what Jesus did for him, he was also a good listener. Because he and Silas were praying and singing hymns, they were connected to God and full of the Holy Spirit. Thus, when the chains came off, they knew they should stay put. I believe the Holy Spirit told them to stay put, and they listened.

5. Read Acts 12:5-10 in your Bible. When Peter's chains came off, did he stay put or did he leave the prison?

I believe that Paul and Silas no doubt had heard about Peter's miraculous escape. When their own chains fell, it would not have been a stretch to assume they should escape too. If not for their connection to God through the Holy Spirit (verse 25), they would not have known what God's desired course of action was in the situation. We can't make an assumption as to what God would have us do based on prior experience. We need to listen every time.

DAY TWO - 7 TIPS FOR SUCCESS

Most people will tell you that you should never talk about religion or politics with people you don't know. Why? Because those are topics that tend to push buttons and ruffle feathers. Evangelizing is not about arguing. As I said earlier, God does not need you to fight for Him. He fought the battle. He needs witnesses willing to declare the truth with love and

4: YOU AREN'T IN A BIBLE DRILL

If you've been through Sunday school classes, you've likely gone through Bible drills. The teacher calls out a verse and the first person to find it, wins.

"I know my Bible better than you do!"

Evangelizing isn't a Bible drill. Remember, the person you are speaking with may not have any reference for lending credibility to the Bible. Throwing verses at them will simply be building a wall. Tell them the concepts of Scripture as they've played out in your own life. Give them something to connect to. If a particular verse is relevant to share, give them a personal story that shows Scripture in action. Don't give the Scripture and leave them guessing how it applies. Evangelizing is about encouragement. Speak of the hope, healing, help, love, salvation that Jesus brought to you.

4. What Bible verses hold special meaning to your life? Why? What aspect of Jesus's character do those verses make come alive in your life?

5: YOU AREN'T IN A SCHOOL PLAY

Just like I don't think a canned Scripture recital is a good idea, I don't think a canned recitation of your testimony is the way to go, either. You need to know your story inside and out, forwards and backwards, so that you can present the parts that will resonate with the person you are speaking with. Yes, it is all about your salvation, but make your story relevant to the other person. If you memorize your testimony and recite it word for word the same way every time, you will seem impersonal and distant.

5. At the end of this book, I am going to encourage you to write out your testimony. If you have previously written it out, I'd like you to get it, and read through what you'd written in years past. Reflect and recall any times you've had to share that testimony and thank God for your salvation story.

Week 5: Becoming Disciples

6: YOU DON'T KNOW ...

Making assumptions about what the other person is thinking or about the meaning of the words they say is risky business. I've learned this one the hard way. When someone says something that sparks a reaction in you, before you respond, clarify, clarify, clarify! A question as simple as, "What do you mean by that?" can avoid confusion in your understanding of what they believe. Ask for more information before you respond. When it comes to evangelizing, the more you know about the other person's state of mind, the easier it will be for you to find the common ground that will open the door for you to speak words of truth and life.

6. Think of an example of a comment someone could make about their faith or about a belief about Jesus that could be misunderstood if you didn't ask for more information.

7: YOU MUST KEEP YOUR EYE ON THE PRIZE

When evangelizing, your job is not to "make converts." Your job is to present the truth of who Christ is. You don't do the saving, Christ does. If you have a respectful, loving, truth-filled conversation with someone and you get to share what Jesus did for you, but that person does not turn and repent during that conversation, you must not take your eye off the prize.

I've had conversations with people where at the beginning I thought I would be sharing the gospel, but during the course of the conversation I realize (through revelation from the Holy Spirit and as I listen to the other person) that what the person before me needs most in that moment is prayer and encouragement. When that happens I lay aside my "agenda" to share the gospel and instead say something like, "I'm sorry you are going through that. Can I pray with you, right now?" I might offer words of encouragement from Scripture, or I may simply pray and ask what I can do for them.

Know and trust this: If that person does not give his or her life to Christ at the end of your conversation, God will send other messengers to further cultivate the seed you've planted. Pray for the person you spoke with. Pray that another messenger will see that person give his or her life to the Lord. If the person is someone you see again, continue to cultivate the seed yourself as God gives you the opportunity. Your goal is to glorify God by doing the things He asks of you. He'll take care of the results as He will, in His time. Your call is obedience to the task.

THE PROSTITUTE'S STORY

In the late 90s, I attended a large church in North Carolina. I had a reputation for street evangelism, as I would frequently go downtown where the prostitutes, pimps, homeless people, and drug dealers were. I would bring them sandwiches and bottled water and would talk to them while they ate.

Once, a couple of women in the college and career ministry of the church wanted to go out on the streets with me to witness and build their evangelism skills. I took them to an area where I had occasionally had the chance to minister.

There were three prostitutes standing together talking on a corner. I pointed them out to my evangelists-in-training and encouraged them to go and strike up a conversation. They walked up to them and two of the prostitutes began to speak to them. The third backed off about ten feet. I stayed back and watched.

They started to tell the street women that Christ loved them. They talked for about twenty minutes, after which the two prostitutes politely said, "Thank you for your time," and they walked off. The third prostitute stuck around. My friends from church thought maybe she wanted to talk, so they began to speak to her. She wasn't interested in talking. She was interested in verbally attacking them, letting them know exactly what she thought of their Jesus. She was hateful and ugly and used language I won't repeat in this book.

As she continued her verbal assault, the two women from my church went into a bit of shock. I don't think they'd heard that kind of language before, and I am certain they'd never heard anyone say those kinds of things about Christ. I didn't know the prostitute's intentions, so I stepped in between them all. A strong feeling of authority came over me. I knew, in that moment, I was up against an evil force at work and I felt rising up in me a holy anger at the words this woman spoke against Christ.

I admonished her for lashing out at two people who were doing nothing but acting respectfully toward her and who were trying to help her better her situation. I told her that because she was so belligerent and rejecting of what had been offered to her, that one day she would stand before God and He would remind her that she rejected Him. I told her that once she was dead, it would be too late to change her mind about Jesus. I told her, "You never know when you will get your last chance to accept Jesus."

She was taken back, and stopped yelling, but hostility oozed from her face and body language. I turned around and we left.

The next morning, I had the news on while I was getting ready for church. A report caught my attention. Police found a body down near the river. It was a female who had been strangled to death. They put up a mug shot of the woman found dead. It was the prostitute from the night before. When I saw her face, I felt a physical and spiritual ache inside. It was the one who violently rejected Jesus when we tried to tell her that He loved her. The one, who a mere 5 hours before she died, I told that she would one day stand before God and it would be too late.

I share this story to illustrate that there may be times when you are aggressively verbally attacked. I wasn't about to stand around and debate with this woman. I wasn't about to get into a fight with her. I did however let her know that rejecting God has eternal consequences. I told her Jesus loved her and we were just trying to help her understand that. And then we walked away.

This story also highlights the importance of preparation and prayer. You can't walk into a situation up against people who call the streets "home" without a whole lot of prayer surrounding you. Those people are battling demons every day, and that spiritual battle may be one you've never experienced yourself. Remember our lesson from Ephesians 6. Put on the spiritual armor of God each and every morning.

DAY THREE - BEFORE, AFTER, STILL CHANGING

> Then Paul stretched out his hand and proceeded to make his defense.
>
> Acts 26:1

Have you ever met a really great storyteller? Great storytellers have mastered the art of building suspense, pausing for emphasis, and recognizing the natural ebb and flow of a tale. When a good story is over, you are left saying, "Wow!"

The apostle Paul was a fabulous storyteller. In Acts 26, Paul shares his testimony with King Agrippa. The Jews had Paul thrown in jail for his faith. The Romans didn't really understand why the Jews had Paul thrown in prison, and King Agrippa wanted to hear Paul speak for himself. With that background, turn to Acts 26 in your Bible and read the entire account.

1. In which verses of Acts 26 does Paul describe how he was before he knew the truth of who Jesus was?

2. In which verses does Paul describe the events of his conversion to Christianity?

3. In which verses does Paul explain how his life has changed since he acknowledged Jesus as Lord over his life?

Week 5: Becoming Disciples

I'm going to give you the answers, because I don't want you to miss this. When Paul tells Agrippa his story, he begins by sharing how he felt about Jesus before he became a Christian. He lays this groundwork in verses 1-11. Then, beginning in verse 12, he tells Agrippa what happened to him that changed his life. He tells his "meeting Jesus" story. Beginning in verse 19, he then goes on to show Agrippa what God is doing now in his life. He shares his passion and his new life mission.

Just like Paul, you have a before, after, and still changing story. I cannot stress enough how important it is for you to not only know your story, but to be able to identify the major people and events that God used to shape and mold you spiritually. God is continually at work in His people. Each milestone, big and small, has the opportunity for you to show God's glory. When you have taken the time to identify how God is at work in your life, you will be ready to share the right components of your story that will matter to the person you are evangelizing to.

I WAS THIS ...

THIS IS HOW I MET JESUS ...

AND NOW I AM THIS ...

4. Does King Agrippa accept Jesus as his Lord in this account? (hint: read verses 26-32)

5. How does Paul respond in verse 29?

6. Do you think Paul's testimony made King Agrippa and the other Roman officials think? Why or why not?

YOUR BEFORE, AFTER, AND STILL CHANGING STORY

Hopefully the text shift didn't throw you off too much. Our next task is to build a timeline of your story, and I wanted to make it as easy as possible for you to read the instructions while you work on the next page.

1. Make a point on the timeline that represents your age when you accepted Christ.

2. Think of key events or turning points in your life. This can include things like: accomplishments, changing schools, going to college, moving to new cities, key relationships (beginning and end of relationships), illnesses or injuries, employment, birth of children, death of someone close, major purchases, missions trips. Mark these events on your timeline. Basically, I want you to think of those things, big and small, joyous and painful, that impacted you.

3. Highlight any event that you think was significant as contributing to your coming to know Jesus as Lord.

4. For any major events that happened AFTER you accepted Christ, make a list on page 100 as to how your relationship with Christ sustained you or strengthened you during that time.

5. For any major events that happened BEFORE you accepted Christ, make a list on page 100 as to how, upon reflection, you can see God's hand was upon your life.

6. If you accepted Christ at a young age, you might not remember events, but mark the relationships that were significant in bringing you to a saving knowledge of Christ.

7. On page 100, think of the Scriptures that God has used at different parts of your story to encourage, exhort, equip, or help you endure that part of your story. Write the references on page 100 and write them on your timeline.

TIMELINE

Today

Your birth

KEY SCRIPTURES THAT HELPED ME:

MAJOR EVENT	HOW CHRIST SUSTAINED / STRENGTHENED ME	SCRIPTURE

Week 5: Becoming Disciples

DAY FOUR - URGENCY AND CHOICES

SAM'S STORY

My son, Ben, just turned ten years old. For his birthday, he asked some friends over for a party then sleepover. Out of everyone he invited, only one kid, Sam, was able to stay overnight. Everyone else went home when the party was over. My wife and I quickly realized why God might have given us this opportunity to have some one on one time with this boy.

First, Sam was wearing one of the What Jesus Did silicone wristbands that we sell as an evangelism tool for the ministry. Ben had given it to him previously. He showed it to us proudly when he got to our house. He said he knew that W.J.D. stood for "What Jesus Did," but wasn't sure what that meant. Then later, when we prayed before dinner, he said he sometimes prayed before eating, but he wasn't sure if he was a Christian. With all the other kids present, it wasn't the right time to talk, but Kim and I both felt strongly that we needed to have a heart to heart talk with him sometime while he was in our home.

At breakfast the next morning, I took the opportunity. I guided the conversation to gauge Sam's understanding of right and wrong, because that is foundational to understanding good and evil. I said, "Let's play a game. I'm going to say something, and you tell me if it is right or wrong."

After 5 questions I knew that he knew right from wrong. From there, I told him that the things we've done wrong in our lives have separated us from God. I told him those things were called sin, and that everybody had sin in their lives.

I asked Sam if he'd ever burned himself on anything. I told him to imagine the pain of a burn, but all over your body, and you are not able to have any relief from it. Here on earth we can put cold water or salve on a burn. In hell, there is no escaping the pain. You must endure the torture, all over yourself, inside and out, for all of eternity. And it isn't just the pain that's bad. There is the smell of burning flesh. I told him straight up, that is what hell is like, and hell is the punishment for our sins when we die.

Our kitchen table is a large, square shape. We were sitting at opposite ends. I stretched my hand toward him and said, "Even though you and I are sitting across the table from each other right now, if we each reach our arms out, we can't touch each other. He stretched his arm out toward me. There was a space between. We couldn't touch. I said, "That's what sin does. It disconnects us from God and creates a big gap, that on our own we can't close."

As we were sitting there I said, "God realized that something had to bridge that gap and connect us back to Him. Sin created a debt in our life. Kind of like a credit card. If you have a credit card, you get a bill every month that tells you how much you have to pay. Sin is like that, but if you got a "sin card" in the mail, you'd never be able to pay it off. God sent Jesus to earth to pay the debt for all of us. Everyone has sinned. But Jesus was perfect, blameless."

I then described Jesus's death on the cross. I explained in detail how he was crucified. I told Sam that it brought a lot of pain to Jesus, but He knew He had to do it. As He hung there, on that cross, with His arms stretched out, it was as if Jesus screamed, "I love you, Sam! And I'm doing this because you can't." I told Sam that Jesus did something no man's ever done. They put Him in a tomb, and three days later He arose. Jesus showed himself to people for several days after rising and then He said, "I must go home to heaven now, but one day, I'm coming back." Right there, Jesus made a way.

I had Ben reach one hand out to me and then reach out to Sam. Ben connected Sam and I. I said, "What Jesus did for us is like what Ben just did. If I was God, and Ben was Jesus, you would be connected to me through Ben."

I said, "Because Jesus came to bridge that gap, you now have a choice. You can ask Jesus to come into your life, which gives you eternity in heaven. Or you can reject Jesus, and you will spend eternity in hell, like how I described to you."

Then I said, "Which one do you want?"

He said, "I want heaven. I want Jesus."

I said, "Would you like to pray and ask Jesus to come into your life right now?"

He said, "Yes."

And together with my son, we prayed and Sam asked Jesus to come live in his heart and change him.

Week 5: Becoming Disciples

I've said earlier in this book that we can't make disciples of Christ if we never give people the chance to become disciples. There are two components to helping people become disciples that most Christians shy away from:

1. Creating a sense of urgency for the person they are speaking with.

2. Actually giving the person the chance to make the choice to follow Jesus.

I had a seminary professor tell me once that it takes, "Seven or more times for someone to hear the gospel before they make the decision to follow Christ."

Now, that may be the North American average, but I can tell you, in places that I've been like China, Africa, India, Malaysia, Thailand, and others, I've seen people come to know Christ the very first time they're given the chance to do so. Nowhere in Scripture do we read that multiple presentations of the gospel are to be expected.

I begin the conversation expecting that the person will decide to give their life to Christ. If they don't, then I have the confidence that I've planted the good seed, and I pray for the Lord to bring others to cultivate it further. But I never start off thinking God isn't ready to do a miracle right then and there, because tomorrow is promised to no one.

Why should there be such an urgency when it comes to salvation? Here is is: 10 out of 10 people will die.

Out of those 10 people, all 10 will go either to heaven or to hell.

No one knows when they will die. Only God knows. But it is our responsibility to be ready.

And working together with Him, we also urge you not to receive the grace of God in vain. For He says, "AT THE ACCEPTABLE TIME I LISTENED TO YOU, AND ON THE DAY OF SALVATION I HELPED YOU." Behold, now is "THE ACCEPTABLE TIME," behold, now is "THE DAY OF SALVATION "

2 Corinthians 6:1-2

---

1. In Acts 2, Peter, now full of the Holy Spirit, stood up and declared to all the men of Judea the truth of who Christ was. This is the same Peter who previously denied even knowing Jesus! Once the Holy Spirit gave him the power, he could not shut up about Jesus. It's time for Christians to stop shutting up and start standing up and speaking up. Read Acts 2:14-40. How did the Jews respond to Peter's declaration? (v 37)

2. What did Peter tell them they were being saved from? (v 40)

3. Read the following. What does each reveal about people and their place in heaven?

Philippians 4:3

Psalm 69:28

Luke 10:20

Exodus 32:33

Revelation 20:11-15

4. When you give someone the choice to accept Jesus, what are you asking them to choose between?

Week 5: Becoming Disciples

Accepting Jesus as Lord and Savior brings salvation from eternal hell. I can't imagine why anyone would NOT choose Jesus, when hell is the other option. But here are some other benefits that people are choosing when they choose Jesus:

Peace versus fear (John 14:27)
Worry-free versus anxieties (1 Peter 5:7)
Hope versus hopelessness (Romans 15:13)
Power versus weakness (Isaiah 40:29)
Light burden versus heavy burden (Matthew 11:30)
Love versus hate (John 3:16)
Self-Control versus no control (1 Corinthians 10:13)
Ability to live godly versus ungodly life (Titus 2:11-14)

Physical death is imminent for all of us. Spiritual death in hell is imminent for those who don't know Jesus. My prayer for you is that you are realizing that the battle being fought in this world has eternal consequences. Many people have never given dutiful thought to that fact.

Christians are far too are complacent and weak when it comes to letting others know that if they were to die, right now, they will stand before God and He will judge them according to one simple question, "Did you accept my Son, Jesus as your Lord and Savior?"

The same Christian who raises her hands to the sky and declares with certainty "Jesus is Lord!" in the pews on Sunday, becomes a wimp about declaring the same thing to a neighbor or friend who doesn't know Christ. Let's stop being spiritual wimps.

Evangelizing is:

1. Listening to the other person's story.

2. Identifying parts that you can connect with.

3. Sharing your testimony in a relevant way.

4. Presenting the gospel.

5. Offering the choice for the person to accept Christ.

Questions for Group Discussion:

Always begin your small group time with prayer.

1. When you were talking to the person who led you to the Lord, what was the thing they said, or the question they asked, that made all the difference for you? What sparked the sense of urgency in you to make a decision to turn your life over to Christ?

2. As you look back over your timeline, who were the key people who encouraged you along the way to make choices that aligned with God's word? Are there qualities they have that you can learn from?

3. Look at the 5 components of evangelism I listed along the right side of page 105. Which of those 5 are you most comfortable living out? How can you improve in the areas where you feel weak?

4. Think of three people in your life who don't know Jesus. Based on what you know about them, what parts of your timeline and your story would most resonate with them?

WEEK SIX
YEAH, BUT ...

Up to this point, I hope you are developing a clearer picture that sharing Jesus is all about opening yourself up to share what Jesus did for you. The Scriptures you study, your preparation time with God, your intentional pursuit of a passionate love for Christ will all come together beautifully as you step into your role as a disciple maker.

In case you missed it, I want to say again, you must have a passionate love for Jesus Christ. That passionate love was given to you when He died for you. Once that love is blazing, you won't be able to help yourself from telling others about Him.

Evangelizing starts with listening to whoever God's placed before you. You learn what you can about their story, so you can appropriately share the parts of your story that will resonate with them. Then, when the Holy Spirit prompts you, you can give them the choice to accept the Jesus that will bring them peace and salvation.

Unfortunately, no matter how good you become at working through that process, when sharing about Jesus you are going to get your fair share of, "Yeah, but..." in response. When someone begins a sentence

> Remember, just as passionately as you want to share Christ, there will be those people who are just as passionate about denouncing or denying God's work on earth.
>
> Atheists, agnostics, and worldly pagans will get fired up to tell you why Jesus *isn't* real.
>
> God gives us an answer for this through Paul's letter to Timothy:
>
> But you, keep your head in all situations, endure hardship, do the work of an evangelist, discharge all the duties of your ministry.
>
> 2 Timothy 4:5 (NIV)

with, "Yeah, but..." I know that whatever comes next out of their mouth is going to be an excuse.

"Yeah, but God wouldn't want someone like me."

"Yeah, but I was raised in a church so I am already a Christian."

"Yeah, but what would my friends think?"

Some, maybe even most, people will resist change. Humans are creatures of habit.

In this week's lesson we are going to look at four of the most common excuses I hear from people who want to hang onto their old ways.

1. Yeah, but the God in the Bible is mean and vengeful.

2. Yeah, but all roads lead to heaven.

3. Yeah, but I won't have any more fun if I become a Christian.

4. Yeah, but I knew you when...

Don't let other people's excuses silence you. You must persevere during difficult days and times. The verse from 2 Timothy that I listed to the left is one I lean on often, especially when evangelizing is discouraging because of other people's excuses. I have a burning passion to see lost people come to know the Jesus who saved me from destruction. I know if it wasn't for Jesus, I'd be dead right now. Physically dead and also in hell, suffering forever. Instead, I have beauty, love, light, and hope for eternity. I don't want anyone to miss out on what God is waiting to give them.

Week 6: Yeah, But ...

DAY ONE - YOU DON'T KNOW BO

In 1989 / 90, Nike ran a genius ad campaign that featured pro-athlete Bo Jackson. Bo played both football and baseball professionally in the same year, and Nike capitalized on his cross-athleticism to make popular the phrase "Bo knows..." (Bo knows football, Bo knows baseball, and Bo knows a whole lot of other things.)

ESPN did a mini-documentary titled *You Don't Know Bo* to give a behind the scenes look at Bo Jackson, using the clever title to play on the "Bo knows" campaign. I still use that phrase to let someone know that although they may "think" they know something, they don't have a clue.

"You don't know Bo!"

When evangelizing, you will come across people who think they know everything there is to know about Jesus. I mean, I've had conversations with people who talk like they have written the Bible themselves. But I know they don't know Jesus. And I know they don't have a clue.

Know-it-alls can be very difficult to evangelize to because:

1. They like to hear themselves talk.

2. They use their words as a defense mechanism against hearing the truth.

3. They don't think they need to change their mind about anything.

One of the ways a know-it-all will try and throw a curve ball at a Christian is to say something like:

"How can you say God loves us when He lets so many bad things happen in this world?"

Yes, people want to blame God for the ugliness here on earth. When someone goes into a school and starts shooting children, God did not tell them to do that. God did not put a gun in the hands of a killer.

God does not condone hate between people on earth. The God who sent Jesus to die for everyone did not support the men who were responsible for the 9-11 terrorist acts. He does not approve of any of the crimes and horrific acts we commit against one another. The ugliness in this world did not come from God. It came from Satan.

Remember on day 3 of week 3 I told you that Satan hates you with a hate so ferocious that he will do whatever it takes to destroy you? Keep that in mind as you work through these questions.

1. If you were asked right now, "Why didn't God create a world that was without suffering, tragedy, or pain?" how would you answer?

2. Read Genesis 1:31. What did God say about what He created?

Week 6: Yeah, But ...

3. Read Genesis 3. Whose choice was it to disobey God?

Adam and Eve first chose to disobey God. God didn't force them to. They knew the consequences of their action would wreck God's perfect creation. Because man allowed sin into the world, sin will dominate in the world until Jesus returns.

4. These things I have spoken to you, so that in Me you may have peace. In the world you have tribulation, but take courage; I have overcome the world. (John 16:33)

According to this verse, how does Jesus say we are to endure the problems in the world?

5. For we know that the whole creation groans and suffers the pains of childbirth together until now. (Romans 8:22)

Who is suffering?

6. The Lord is not slow about His promise, as some count slowness, but is patient toward you, not wishing for any to perish but for all to come to repentance. (2 Peter 3:9)

Why do you think, after reading this verse, that Jesus hasn't returned to right the wrongs of this world yet?

Journaling

Jesus answered, "It was neither that this man sinned, nor his parents; but it was so that the works of God might be displayed in him."

John 9:3

This verse is one that God gave to Kim to show her that through our son's autism, we can bring glory to Him. It brought healing in her heart and she uses it often to encourage other parents in our similar situation.

Journal about something in your life that the world may perceive as bad, but you know God can use for the good of others.

My oldest son has autism. I've held my wife as she wept over the struggles autism brings sometimes. But we both realize that God didn't allow him to have autism because God is cruel, or because God doesn't love us. Whatever happened when his tiny self was developing that caused his autism is because we live in a fallen world. But, through his autism, Kim and I have an amazing opportunity to show others how big of a God we serve. We can bring glory to God through our sufferings and show others that they can have peace in their trials, too.

God does not treat us like puppets. We can choose whether we will stay faithful to His promises, even during our difficulties, or not. When we do, He promises us we will have peace.

When I am asked, "Why does God allow bad things to happen?" I always go first to the fact that each one of us has sinned. I ask them, "Have you ever lied? Stolen something? Cheated? Done even worse things?"

Of course they have. Because ALL have sinned. And because we have all sinned, we all have to bear the consequences of living in a fallen world. But then I go on to explain that Jesus has provided the way out.

Why didn't God create a world without tragedy or pain? He did! We're the ones who messed it up. He will right it again, but until the day and time when He rises and declares, "Enough!" He is waiting patiently for all to have the chance to repent and accept Jesus.

Week 6: Yeah, But ...

DAY TWO - NOT ALL ROADS LEAD TO HEAVEN

I once asked a man who was in his fifties what he thought would happen after he dies.

"Well, I think pretty much everyone goes to heaven," he replied.

"What do you mean 'pretty much everyone'?" I asked.

"The really bad people will go to hell, but I think God lets the good people in," he said.

"How does God decide who is good enough?" I asked.

"You know, keeping the ten commandments, not murdering, stuff like that," he said.

"How did you come to this conclusion?" I asked. "Because that isn't what God says in the Bible."

"Look," he said. "You believe what you want and I'll believe what I want. At the end of the day, all the good people will end up in heaven. And if God doesn't want me, well then screw Him."

I come across some variation of this thinking quite often. People believe that all religions, all beliefs, all faiths, will lead to some sort of heaven. Do all roads lead to heaven? My theological answer is a big, fat NO!

But you probably want a little more substance to help you when you are asked that same question. If you think about it logically, it is impossible for every road to lead to heaven. All faiths, all belief systems, all claims cannot be true. Why? Because they contradict each other.

Jesus said, "I am the way, and the truth, and the

life; no one comes to the Father but through Me." (John 14:6) The use of the capital "M" in "Me" indicates the person Jesus. He is stating that the only way to get to God, and eternal life, is through Him and Him alone.

The Bible says that we can NOT get to heaven on the basis of our works. As I showed you in week 4, other religions base your worthiness on doing good deeds.

1. Highlight or circle how the verses below say that we are saved:

For by grace you have been saved through faith; and that not of yourselves, it is the gift of God; not as a result of works, so that no one may boast. (Ephesians 2:8-9)

We believe it is through the grace of our Lord Jesus that we are saved, just as they are. (Acts 15:11)

And all are justified freely by his grace through the redemption that came by Christ Jesus. (Romans 3:24)

It does not, therefore, depend on human desire or effort, but on God's mercy. (Romans 9:16)

Islam, Hindu, J.W., and Mormon faiths all say that if you are not a part of their "religion" you cannot get to heaven. So even they don't claim that "all roads lead to heaven."

Christians recognize Jesus's resurrection. Other faiths deny this event took place. Muhammad, and the prophets of these other false religions are all lying dead in their graves. The bottom line is that someone is right and everybody else is wrong. All roads can't lead to heaven, because everybody isn't right.

"So, how do I know that Christianity is the true

Week 6: Yeah, But ...

religion and the others are the false ones?" you might be asked.

To address this, I go back again to the historical accuracy of the Bible as opposed to the man-made religions, all of which began hundreds of years after Christ walked the earth. More importantly, I tell people that I know my faith is real because I've experienced Jesus's power in my life. I've seen who I was before and I know who I am now.

2. All roads do not lead to heaven in the sense that everyone is allowed access in. BUT, no matter what you believe here on earth, you will end up standing before God when you die. So I suppose in a sense all roads will get you to the door, but only Jesus is the key to get in.

If you think about this, and the other things we discussed, how would you answer if someone said to you the things the man said to me in the opening to today's lesson?

DAY THREE - THE PARTY'S NOT OVER!

I don't know why people equate Christianity to a lifestyle of doom and gloom, but I occasionally hear, "If I give my life to Jesus, I won't have any more fun!" I like to say those people have the "Vegas mentality." The Vegas mentality is that "What happens in Vegas, stays in Vegas." Basically it means that whatever drinking, partying, sex, or other debauchery you do can be contained and put away as if it never happened, until you decide to do it again.

I lived that lifestyle. Looking back, it wasn't

fun. I can't tell you how many mornings I woke up, couldn't remember what happened the night before, later had recollections (or friends reminded me) that I made a fool of myself, and then, laying there in agony, I said, "I will never drink again, if I survive this!"

1. What do you think people are referring to when they say, "Christianity doesn't sound like fun" or "I won't have fun anymore if I become a Christian"?

MY STORY

I'm going to go back to my own testimony for a bit here, because it shows you well my personal experience with this objection. On the day I accepted Christ, I woke up feeling two steps away from death. I woke up on my living room floor. I had a horrible headache. I felt terrible. I knew, as I lie there, that there had to be more to life than drinking, drugs, and causing trouble. That was why I threw the challenge out to God to prove Himself to me that day. The party life was not fulfilling. It was killing me.

When I accepted Christ, it was as if a crushing burden, a heavy spiritual weight was lifted off of me. I still had wants, but my wants changed. I no longer wanted to drink, I didn't want to do drugs, I didn't want to fight or cause pain to others. I wanted to wake up in the morning feeling good. I wanted to wake up and not worry that the police were going to come knocking because of something stupid I'd done.

I wanted to finally experience love, because I never had, except through my mom.

Accepting Christ didn't make the party end. Accepting Christ allowed the party to begin. What the world views as a party, is so much less than what God really has in store for you. God doesn't want to stifle us, He wants to help us live to the fullest.

God created you. He gave you talents, special gifts, likes and dislikes. He gave you these things so you can enjoy them, as you declare His glory. That's your sweet spot. When we are full of alcohol or drugs, we can't use our gifts for God. When we are full of any selfish, "me-pleasing," thoughts, we aren't going to be focused on God's best for us. When someone says, "I won't have any fun if I become a Christian," what I believe they are saying is, "I don't want to give up control of my agenda, my selfish wants, and pleasing myself." That's a sad way to live life. I know. I tried it.

2. How did your wants and desires change when you accepted Christ? If you accepted Christ at a young age, then let me ask you, what kinds of things do you want and intentionally pursue? Are they Christ-centered or self-centered things?

3. God has given me a "stick-to-it" personality. He has given me a fierce loyalty and strong tenacity for those things that matter to me. He's given me the ability to feel comfortable talking with strangers. He's given me a passion for the underdog. I used to use those talents to cause trouble. I got fiercely passionate about the wrong things. I used my "talk to stranger" ability to sell drugs. But once I gave my life to Christ and my wants changed, those same talents now contribute to my ability to evangelize boldly. So let me ask you, what things are you good at? What talents has God given you? Can you see how God has given your gifts to bring Him glory? List them, so you can share them as part of your story to testify as to how God created you to do good works.

If someone you speak to is clinging to something they think they have to "give up" in order to follow Christ, I would speak to them about God as their Creator. God made them to do good things here. He made them with gifts and talents. He gave them

> The thief comes only to steal and kill and destroy; I came that they may have life, and have it abundantly.
>
> John 10:10

things they are good at. And I would explain that when we cling to selfish things, we aren't using our gifts to the fullest. Eventually, we will be left feeling "purposeless" because we aren't doing what we were made to do.

The things we think are fun on a worldly level come with consequences. All that fun will catch up with you. Diseases, broken relationships, broken hearts, depression, even death. The Bible warns against seeking temporal, worldly pleasure. God's rules aren't there to stifle your fun. That kind of thinking comes from Satan. Satan is a joy-stealer. He hates you, remember? And he knows that the world's pleasures will eventually destroy you.

DAY FOUR - I KNEW YOU WHEN

> Therefore if anyone is in Christ, he is a new creature; the old things passed away; behold, new things have come.
>
> 2 Corinthians 5:17

Once it becomes known that you have a renewed passion for evangelism, many of you are going to run into a brick wall. What I mean is you're going to have to share with those who knew you B.C. (before Christ!)

One thing you'll learn quickly is the hardest people to share your faith with are those who are family or friends. It is hard because they know all (or most) of what you've ever done wrong. Even if you've been a long-time believer, you've still made mistakes in life and your family and friends know it.

Non-believer family and friends already have more than enough ammo to shoot back at you when you begin to explain why they need a relationship with Jesus.

Here is how to handle it. Take a deep breath, smile, and agree with them. Yes, what you may have

Week 6: Yeah, But ...

done in the past is bad. But, you can explain, that is exactly why you need Christ in your life: To make you new. To help you become more like Him.

1. Look up the following verses in your Bible. What does each say about who you are with Christ in your life or how you are to handle your past?

Isaiah 43:18-19

Ezekiel 36:26

Romans 6:4

Ephesians 4:23-24

You don't just have a "newfound religion" you have a new heart! A new mind! A new self! That is exciting. You can tell that to the person who is giving you the "I knew you when..." speech. Let them know you are a work in progress, then share how Christ is helping you overcome the things of the past.

2. Who do you think will be the hardest person in your family or close circle of friends to share the gospel with? Why?

3. What things from your past do you think your family and friends will throw back in your face when you try to share about Jesus?

4. Knowing how you will feel if and when your past is brought up to you, what is the best way to act? Remember, they want to drag you back to your old flesh.

5. Have you had conversations with family members that tend to go down the "same old path" and end up in an argument? We touched on this earlier in the study, but now I want you to really reflect on what you can do to break that bondage. Those old patterns that end in hurt are exactly what Satan wants you to do, in order to keep people from moving closer to Jesus.

Week 6: Yeah, But ...

Questions for Group Discussion:

Always begin your small group time with prayer.

1. Refer back to your timeline. Is there a place of pain on your timeline that you blamed God for your suffering? Even if was a temporary blaming God, it is significant to identify your feelings around that time. It may be a story you can share with someone who doesn't know Christ, but is going through a similar mindset, wondering why God allowed something to happen. How did you work out your feelings? What Scriptures did you turn to?

2. Do you know someone who is clinging to the world for fear that life in Christ isn't that much fun? What would you say to that person if he/she was in front of you right now?

3. What are the "worldly wants" that Satan tempts you with? How do you fight the temptation to put on the old self?

4. Spend time as a group in deep, intentional prayer for those in your family and inner circle of friends who don't know Jesus. Commit to supporting one another in your group in prayer this week for those people.

WEEK SEVEN
MAKING DISCIPLES

Is there anything that would prevent you right now from accepting the gift that Jesus offers?

Each question I've asked you in this book has been done for the purpose of allowing you to see all of the different parts of your story and get you thinking as to how you can use them intentionally as you share the gospel.

I pray that you haven't rushed over them, and have taken the time to think about each one. Not every person needs to hear every part of your story, but **you** need to know your story clearly. I've heard people flounder as they've tried to tell their testimony. It isn't that they don't know Jesus, they've never practiced articulating what Jesus did for them.

Your history, your experiences, your uniqueness, all have relevance to different people at different times. For example, when my wife and I are talking with someone who is a parent of a child with special needs, we talk about what God has done for us as parents of a child with special needs. We relate to the people we speak with on relevant terms.

When we've gone to minister at the Olympics, my wife draws from her gymnastics background and I draw from my soccer background when speaking to athletes about the difference Christ makes in the life of an athlete.

You, too, have unique stories that God will want

to use at different times, with different people. That's why I asked you so many "Recall a time when ..." questions. Look back through those questions often. Review and prayerfully study your timeline. Ask God to show you the glory He can be given through your experiences.

These last four days of study will bring it all together as we investigate what comes next, after you've given the person the chance to accept Jesus as Lord and Savior. You've given someone the chance to become a disciple. Now, we will look at making disciples.

As you can tell from the evangelism examples I've shared throughout this book, I usually ask the person some version of the question, "Is there any reason you have for not accepting Jesus, right here, right now?"

I pray God gives you so many opportunities to ask that question that you lose count!

We spoke in earlier lessons that there will be those people who outright reject the message of Christ or who simply do not want to hear you talk about your faith. But, there will be those glorious moments God blesses you to lead someone to a saving relationship with Christ. In this last week of study, I would like to talk about how you, as an evangelist, can support those people who are receptive to the message of Christ and how you can leave behind a lasting legacy.

DAY ONE - THE WORK IN PROGRESS

Have you ever seen Mount Rushmore up close? It is amazing. Carving Mount Rushmore didn't happen overnight. The carving work took 6 years to complete and more than 400 people to do it.

It can be frustrating when you have people in your life who you really want to see come to accept Jesus, but they are resisting God's truth. Remember, we are all a work in progress. No one arrives as a nice, polished, finished product. We are not perfect, so there are areas of life where we are incomplete.

There are people in your life who aren't outright rejecting of the gospel, but they waffle when it comes to making a decision. They may ask you about church, or talk to you about their own struggles, but when you declare Jesus as the answer to their need, they won't commit.

As an evangelist, you are to be an encouragement to others, especially those who seem interested in church, but don't know Jesus as Savior yet. That hard-headed person, who continues to have excuses as to why they don't want to accept Christ, needs your encouragement, patience, and consistency. They need to consistently see Jesus as Lord of your life and hear of the great things He is doing for you.

1. Look up the following verses. What does each one say about how you are to conduct yourself and why?

Matthew 5:14-16

Luke 8:16

Acts 13:47

You'll remember in week 1, day 2 of our study (page 16), I asked the question if demonstrating to your neighbors that you live differently, letting coworkers know you don't partake in drinking parties, parenting your children differently, etc. can all be called evangelism?

Well, now I will tell you that, yes, those things are a part of evangelizing. We are called to bring light to this dark world, and the things we choose to do and refrain from doing can help point others to Jesus. Your consistency in how you live your life will be noticed by those around you. When you live consistently for God, and then proclaim what Jesus did for you as the reason for your hope, they will not be able to deny the power of Christ in your life.

2. Thinking back to when you accepted Christ, what fears did you have about giving Jesus control over your life?

3. What helped you get over the hump and decide that Jesus was the answer to your life's problems?

Read the following passage from Genesis 3:1-10

Now the serpent was more crafty than any beast of the field which the Lord God had made. And he said to the woman, "Indeed, has God said, 'You shall not eat from any tree of the garden'?" 2 The woman said to the serpent, "From the fruit of the trees of the garden we may eat; 3 but from the fruit of the tree which is in the middle of the garden, God has said, 'You shall not eat from it or touch it, or you will die.'" 4 The serpent said to the woman, "You surely will not die! 5 For God knows that in the day you eat from it your eyes will be opened, and you will be like God, knowing good and evil." 6 When the woman saw that the tree was good for food, and that it was a delight to the eyes, and that the tree was desirable to make one wise, she took from its fruit and ate; and she gave also to her husband with her, and he ate. 7 Then the eyes of both of them were opened, and they knew that they were naked; and they sewed fig leaves together and made themselves loin coverings.

8 They heard the sound of the Lord God walking in the garden in the cool of the day, and the man and his wife hid themselves from the presence of the Lord God among the trees of the garden. 9 Then the Lord God called to the man, and said to him, "Where are you?" 10 He said, "I heard the sound of You in the garden, and I was afraid because I was naked; so I hid myself.

4. What was the temptation that the serpent laid out before Eve? (verse 5)

5. What three things did the serpent's temptation get Eve excited about?

6. Why did Adam say he and Eve hid from God, after they disobeyed Him?

Week 7: Making Disciples

The person resisting God's call is a lot like Adam and Eve. Adam and Eve wanted to be wise like God. They wanted to have control over things, like God. As a result, when God came close, they became afraid of Him. The person resisting Christ wants to keep that control over their life. They resist giving Him first place over their own desires.

When you present Jesus to this kind of person, there will be a fear, just like Adam and Eve had. You're trying to bring Jesus close, and that scares people. Not because it doesn't sound good, but they are afraid of the unknown. They don't know what God will do if He is in control. The funny thing is, their sense of control is a false one. God is already in control.

A WEALTHY WOMAN'S STORY

Once, while on a mainstream music tour, I had the chance to get to know an extremely wealthy woman and her family. This family is a household name, known for their television and musical endeavors. As God gave me the opportunity, I shared the gospel with her. She looked me in the eye, and with enthusiasm said, "David, that sounds amazing. Accepting Jesus sounds wonderful. But I am afraid if I accept Christ, God will take away everything we've worked so hard to build over the years."

Her fear of losing control over her life kept her from accepting Christ's riches in that moment. When you evangelize to someone like that, let them know, God's already in control. He's waiting to make their life better. When we get with God's program, He promises us a fulfillment and purpose we could never manufacture on our own. Persevere with the "works in progress" God puts before you. Keep living well, preaching boldly, and praying fervently for them to release their fears to the Lord.

> For He spoke, and it was done; He commanded, and it stood fast. The Lord nullifies the counsel of the nations; He frustrates the plans of the peoples. The counsel of the Lord stands forever, The plans of His heart from generation to generation.
>
> Psalm 33:9-11

DAY TWO - GUIDING THE NEW BELIEVER

Prayer to Receive Christ

Jesus, I come to you today realizing that I am a sinner. The things I've done wrong have separated me from God. I ask you today to forgive me.

I believe you died on the cross for my sins. I believe you rose from the dead, defeating death once for all mankind. Jesus, I want to follow you. I ask you to come into my life and take the place of Lord and Savior. Guide me from this day forward and teach me Your ways.

Amen.

"Yes, I want to accept Jesus right now."

Those are the most glorious words you'll ever hear when you are evangelizing. They mean that someone is about to be snatched from Satan's clutches and placed into God's hands, where that person will remain for eternity.

When someone desires to accept Christ, I tell them that I am going to pray out loud, and they can repeat the words that I say. But, (and this is a big BUT) you must tell them that the power is not in the words that they say. Salvation comes because they've had a change of heart about their sin and they have realized that they need Jesus.

You'll hear that prayer of salvation referred to as a "sinner's prayer." Basically, it provides the person the opportunity to declare that they understand not only what Jesus did for them, but they acknowledge that Jesus is going to help them as they move forward. Let me be clear on something. Nowhere in the book of Acts do we find the apostles leading new believers in a "sinner's prayer." Instead, we find them declaring, "Repent, believe in your heart that Jesus is Lord, and you will be saved."

Praying the prayer is not the thing that saves. You are saved when you have a change of heart about your sin, about who Jesus is, and about your desire to have Him as Lord and Savior over your life. It is the condition of a person's heart, and only God can see that. Praying the prayer can be an outward declaration of the change happening inside.

When Scripture uses the word "heart," it is referring to a person's belief system. Or another way

Week 7: Making Disciples

to say it would be, "Believe at the core of who you are that Jesus is Lord, and you will be saved."

This is important to explain to the person you are praying with. I always ask, "Did you mean that prayer?"

If they say, "Yes," then I say, "Welcome to God's family."

1. A new believer is spiritually a newborn baby. You wouldn't feed a newborn baby a steak. Babies do not have the digestive system to process complex foods. They need simple foods, like milk, and they progress to thicker, more dense foods as they grow. Also, babies don't have the molars to chew meat properly, so if you give a baby a piece of meat, he is likely to choke on it.

Likewise, a new believer will learn and grow in his or her understanding of the nourishment given by the word of God. Read the following verses. Circle the instructions for the believer in Christ. I selected these because I think they are relevant and understandable for the new believer. They give clear instruction as to the things that will build positively into the new believer's life.

Trust in the Lord with all your heart And do not lean on your own understanding. (Proverbs 3:5)

Therefore, putting aside all malice and all deceit and hypocrisy and envy and all slander, like newborn babies, long for the pure milk of the word, so that by it you may grow in respect to salvation, if you have tasted the kindness of the Lord. (1 Peter 2:1-3)

But seek first His kingdom and His righteousness, and all these things will be added to you. (Matthew 6:33)

Be anxious for nothing, but in everything by prayer and supplication with thanksgiving let your requests be made known to God. And the peace of God, which surpasses all comprehension, will guard your hearts and your minds in Christ Jesus. (Philippians 4:6)

I have not departed from the command of His lips; I have treasured the words of His mouth more than my necessary food. (Job 23:12)

So then, those who had received his word were baptized; and that day there were added about three thousand souls. They were continually devoting themselves to the apostles' teaching and to fellowship, to the breaking of bread and to prayer. (Acts 2:41-42)

Regarding baptism, I am often asked three questions:
1. Must a follower of Christ must be baptized?
2. Do I have to be immersed in the water or is sprinkling with water good enough?
3. If I was baptized as a baby, is that the same thing?

My short answer to these questions is, "A believer needs to be baptized by immersion and it should happen after that believer has come to the understanding of who Jesus Christ is as their Savior." Babies cannot make that decision for themselves. Here is my Scriptural teaching that backs this up.

Then Jesus came from Galilee to the Jordan to be baptized by John. 14 But John tried to deter him, saying, "I need to be baptized by you, and do you come to me?" 15 Jesus replied, "Let it be so now; it is proper for us to do this to fulfill all righteousness." Then John consented. 16 As soon as Jesus was baptized, he went up out of the water. At that moment heaven was opened, and he saw the Spirit of God descending like a dove and alighting on him. 17 And a voice from heaven said, "This is my Son, whom I love; with him I am well pleased." (Matthew 3:13-17 *NIV*)

Now John also was baptizing at Aenon near Salim, because there was plenty of water, and people were coming and being baptized. (John 3:23)

As they traveled along the road, they came to some water and the eunuch said, "Look, here is water. What can stand in the way of my being baptized?" [37 Some manuscripts include here Philip said, "If you believe with all your heart, you may."] 38 The eunuch

Week 7: Making Disciples

answered, "I believe that Jesus Christ is the Son of God." 38 And he gave orders to stop the chariot. Then both Philip and the eunuch went down into the water and Philip baptized him. 39 When they came up out of the water, the Spirit of the Lord suddenly took Philip away, and the eunuch did not see him again, but went on his way rejoicing. (Acts 8:36-39)

2. Was Jesus sprinkled with water, or was He baptized by immersion?

3. Did John baptize other people by immersion?

4. Did Philip immerse the eunich in the water? What wording does the Scripture give that indicates this?

The example and instructions Christ gave, combined with the definition of the word baptism as translated from the Greek text, all point to the necessity of baptism by immersion for a believer in Christ.

If you have the chance to continue to connect with the new believer, encourage them often. There are things they will want to change about their life. Remind them they are under construction. Just as Dr. Johnson explained to me, some things will be easier to change, some things will take more time.

Help them, if you can, to find a Bible-teaching church where they can come under the teaching of a good pastor. My definition of a good pastor is one who believes in the Bible as 100% truth and preaches from the word. He doesn't shy away from Scripture and he doesn't preach to make message feel good for the listeners.

And definitely encourage them to begin to tell others what Jesus did for them.

> The Greek word translated baptism is baptizo. It means:
> to dip repeatedly, to immerse, to submerge (of vessels sunk)
> to cleanse by dipping or submerging, to wash, to make clean with water, to wash one's self, bathe
> to overwhelm

5. What are some practical things that you can do to help someone you've had the chance to lead to Christ to take the next steps?

DAY THREE - BE A PAUL, FIND A TIMOTHY

1. List below the names of three people who have had an impact on your spiritual growth, somewhere along the course of your life. Next to each name, write down two things that person did that you remember as contributing to a better understanding of who Christ is.

Person 1: _____   What they did: 1.)
                                                                                                             2.)

Person 2: _____   What they did: 1.)
                                                                                                             2.)

Person 3: _____   What they did: 1.)
                                                                                                             2.)

> As a result, we are no longer to be children, tossed here and there by waves and carried about by every wind of doctrine, by the trickery of men, by craftiness in deceitful scheming; but speaking the truth in love, we are to grow up in all aspects into Him who is the head, even Christ.
>
> Ephesians 4:15

Life with Christ is one of continual growth. We are to grow ourselves, and we are to contribute positively to the growth of our brothers and sisters in Christ. Farmers must cultivate the land in order for maximum growth of the plants. The seed that was planted in the new believer's heart must be given maximum opportunity to grow. Other believers have a responsibility to help that new believer learn how to cultivate their lifestyle for maximum growth. Once someone accepts Christ, their work isn't done. They must join the cause for Christ and become evangelists themselves in order to grow God's kingdom. We must come alongside those who we can to help them fulfill God's call on their life.

Once you disciple someone to become an evangelist, now there are two of you, and you can do twice the work. When they go out and help make disciples, then the numbers double again.

In this day's lesson, we are going to look at how you can intentionally pursue relationships where you are discipling someone in their walk with Jesus.

A few years ago, the word "mentor" became a buzz-word in the church and in corporate America. Everyone was looking for a mentor to provide guidance and life-direction. Then mentors went away and "life coaches" took their place. I am going to talk about a discipling relationship, which some might call mentoring, but I do not want you to think of it in the same way the world looks at mentors and life coaches. A biblical mentor promotes spiritual growth with Jesus, not themselves, as the ultimate example.

If you look at the names of the people I had you list in question 1, each of them contributed toward your spiritual growth. Maybe it was intentional, maybe they contributed simply by their example. But they helped you better understand who Christ is, and you remembered them for it. That's what I mean when I say we need to intentionally pursue discipling relationships.

1. In the verses below, circle the instructions Paul gives to the recipients of his letters.

For you yourselves know how you ought to follow our example, because we did not act in an undisciplined manner among you. (2 Thessalonians 3:7)

The things you have learned and received and heard and seen in me, practice these things, and the God of peace will be with you. (Philippians 4:9)

Be imitators of me, just as I also am of Christ. (1 Corinthians 11:1)

Paul never called himself a "mentor." Rather, he instructed others to look to his example, because he was imitating Christ. He saw himself as one who was to teach, preach, and demonstrate what life in Christ meant.

Timothy was someone who Paul took the time to intentionally teach and help grow in his faith.

2. The Bible records two of the letters Paul wrote to Timothy during their ministry. Below are just a handful of verses from those letters. Read them and circle how Paul showed that he cared about Timothy's growth?

For I am mindful of the sincere faith within you, which first dwelt in your grandmother Lois and your mother Eunice, and I am sure that it is in you as well. (2 Timothy 1:5)

Make every effort to come to me soon. (2 Timothy 4:9)

I thank God, whom I serve with a clear conscience the way my forefathers did, as I continually remember you in my prayers night and day (2 Timothy 1:3)

But the goal of our instruction is love from a pure heart and a good conscience and a sincere faith. (1 Timothy 1:5)

Let no one look down on your youthfulness, but rather in speech, conduct, love, faith and purity, show yourself an example of those who believe. (1 Timothy 4:12)

He considered me faithful, putting me into service, even though I was formerly a blasphemer and a prosecutor and a violent aggressor ... (1 Timothy 1:12(b)-13)

O Timothy, guard what has been entrusted to you, avoiding worldly and empty chatter and the opposing arguments of what is falsely called "knowledge" (1 Timothy 6:20)

Week 7: Making Disciples

These are the things I gained insight into from looking at the things Paul wrote to Timothy:
1. He knew Timothy's family situation and his salvation story.
2. He and Timothy had face to face fellowship.
3. He provided instruction from a place of love.
4. He encouraged Timothy to stand firm in the face of discouragement.
5. He prayed for Timothy continually.
6. He shared his own experiences and stories with Timothy.
7. He warned Timothy against worldly dangers.

Most importantly, he continually pointed Timothy to the Scriptures and to Jesus Christ.

Caring about the spiritual growth of another believer means getting involved in the things of their life. We all start out as Timothys. As you strive to become an imitator of Christ (through prayer, obedience to the word, and being a committed disciple), God will show you your Timothy relationship.

You'll know your Timothy's background and story. You will encourage your Timothy. You'll have face to face fellowship (not just e-mail or texts). You will point your Timothy to Scriptures for instruction. You will be that living example of Christ they can look up to. Ultimately, you'll be preparing your Timothy to go out and become a Paul for someone else.

Who is your Timothy?

That is an excellent question. Begin praying, right now for God to reveal the Timothy He wants you to disciple.

Maybe it is someone at your church, maybe it is someone at work, maybe your Timothy is your son or daughter.

The church today needs more Pauls, who are looking after the spiritual growth of the Timothys in their midst, developing them to become Pauls themselves.

Making disciples doesn't happen by accident, and isn't a job relegated only to pastors. Everyone, male and female, who follows Christ should one day be a Paul to a Timothy.

3. Get a blank journal. When God reveals your Timothy to you, begin to write to your Timothy. As your relationship progresses and you see spiritual growth, record those things. One day, you can give this journal to your Timothy when he or she is ready to become a Paul.

What Jesus Did Bible Study — David Soesbee

DAY FOUR - BEING AN EVANGELIST WHO LEAVES A LEGACY

The Bridge Builder

In this poem, the old man recognizes that someone is coming along behind him who will face the same challenges he has faced.

The old man also recognizes that the youth coming along behind may not be equipped with the same abilities he has. Therefore the old man takes responsibility to help the up and comer be able to safely cross the bridge.

How do you think this can apply to our Christian walk?

An old man, going a lone highway,
Came at evening, cold and gray,
To a chasm, vast and deep and wide,
Through which was flowing a sullen tide.
The old man crossed the twilight dim–
That sullen stream had no fears for him;
But he turned, when he had reached the other side,
He built a bridge to span the tide.

"Old man," said a fellow pilgrim near,
"You are wasting strength building here.
Your journey will end with the ending day;
You never again will pass this way.
You have crossed the chasm, deep and wide,
Why build up the bridge eventide?"

The builder lifted his old gray head.
"Good friend, in the path I have come," he said.
"There followeth after me today
A youth whose feet must pass this way.
This chasm that has been naught to me
To that fair-haired youth may a pitfall be.
He, too, must cross in the twilight dim;
Good friend, I am building the bridge for him."

~ *William Allen Dromgoole*

Week 7: Making Disciples

We are very blessed to have the Scriptures to learn from. There is literally no other book in the world, or in history, besides the Bible that you can turn to and seek out any question you may have in life and you'll find an answer.

As you read the Bible, particularly the New Testament, you will quickly see that once Jesus gave the command to "Go," Paul became the greatest evangelist ever. Think of any evangelist: Billy Graham, D.L. Moody, John Wesley, Jonathan Edwards–all of them have spent hours upon hours reading and studying the teaching of Paul.

Think about this: Paul's conversion dramatically changed the course of his life. He was hell-bound, then he was heaven-bound. BUT, it didn't stop with him. His conversion changed the course for countless lives in his day, and every day since then. TO THIS VERY DAY, Paul's legacy for Christ continues because of his evangelism.

We can only pray that we leave behind a legacy of evangelism as well.

> When you are the light of Christ you can go into places and environments where worldly pleasures dominate and not compromise your faith or your witness.
>
> You must refrain from the temptation to be impacted by the world, instead of impacting the world.
>
> I don't mean you should go looking for trouble. It took 15 years of discipleship under my pastor before God allowed me to cross paths with some of the people who knew me before I was saved. As such, my witness to them was stronger, the change in me was more noticable, and my evangelism skills were sharper.

1. What is the legacy you want to leave behind? What kinds of things do you want to be remembered for?

This Little Light of Mine

This little light of mine,
I'm gonna let it shine.
This little light of mine,
I'm gonna let it shine, let it
shine, let it shine, let it shine.

Won't let Satan blow it out,
I'm gonna let it shine.
Won't let Satan blow it out,
I'm gonna let it shine, let it
shine, let it shine, let it shine.

Let it shine til Jesus comes,
I'm gonna let it shine.
Let it shine til Jesus comes,
I'm gonna let it shine, let it
shine, let it shine, let it shine.

Hide it under a bushel - NO!
I'm gonna let it shine.
Hide it under a bushel - NO!
I'm gonna let it shine, Let it
shine, let it shine, let it shine.

Let it shine over the whole
wide world,
I'm gonna let it shine.
Let it shine over the whole
wide world,
I'm gonna let it shine, let it
shine, let it shine, let it shine.

There is a childhood song embraced by Sunday School teachers all across the world, because of its simple message and catchy tune. *This Little Light of Mine* is one that even non-believers often know.

I would rally behind a petition to make this the official anthem for all followers of Christ. All too often, believers only let their light shine when they are among other believers.

That is like standing outside at noon on a clear and sunny day and shining a flashlight up into the sky. The flashlight is not effective; no one would see its light. The purpose of a flashlight, to give light where there is not light, becomes null. But, if we took that same flashlight out at midnight, wherever we point it would become illuminated. It fulfills its purpose.

That is what a believer should be in this world. When we don't turn our flashlight on at the right time, or we turn it on only in the presence of other Christians, we are not fulfilling our purpose.

In Mark 16:15 Jesus said, "Go into all the world and preach the gospel to all creation."

If you are a follower of Jesus Christ, I don't care if you dig ditches for a living or are the senior pastor of a church, you have been commanded by Jesus to go out and share what Jesus did for you personally, bringing the light of Christ. You are to shine until the day He calls you heavenward.

This is your time to shine. It is your time to intentionally leave behind a legacy for others to follow as you share What Jesus Did for you!

2. If you took an honest assessment of your "light-shining," how often would you say you shine your light in places where light is desperately needed?

3. Paul's salvation story has dramatically changed the lives of others. Who has had the course of their life dramatically changed because of your salvation story?

SUMMARY

Since coming to know Christ, God has allowed me to travel the world. I've been to more than 50 countries, where I've preached the gospel and had the privilege to lead people to a saving relationship with Christ. That excites me. At one youth conference, after I spoke and gave an invitation to come forward to accept Christ, I saw over 700 people make decisions to turn their lives over to Jesus. I was moved to tears.

But what has blessed me the most, in light of the thousands of people I've seen come to know Christ, was that I was there when two of our three children turned their lives over to Jesus. Sharing the gospel with my kids, and seeing them say "yes" to Jesus, was greater than any other salvation story. Our third child accepted Christ with my wife.

Now, our kids' salvation isn't any more special than anyone else's, but what I want you to see is that God has placed people in your house, in your work, in your immediate circle of contact each day, with whom He desires you to shine His light. It is very sweet when someone you love very much comes to know Jesus and you get to be a part of it.

Just because someone is raised in a Christian home, that doesn't mean they are being raised to be evangelistic. Ben was 6 when he accepted Christ (he is 10 now), Kacey was 7, and Cooper was 12. Their story isn't over. It is just beginning. And it is up to my wife and I to disciple them to see Christ at work every day. If you have young kids in your home, and they've prayed to receive Christ, you need to be about the work of showing them how to share their faith. Let them see that you care about sharing your faith. Evangelism doesn't begin when you are an adult. It begins when you become a follower of Christ. One area where I feel churches can do a better job is teaching new believers to talk about how their story has meshed with Jesus's story. When we don't teach new believers how to talk about their faith from early on, they think being a Christian is about becoming a member of a club or society and they end up as, what I like to call, "pew potatoes."

Being an evangelist is being a passionate storyteller. It's storming the gates of hell with Jesus's love. I've strived in writing this study to help you identify how to use the parts of your story to evangelize. I hope I've shown you that when you connect your story with Jesus's story, you offer hope, healing, and heaven for the person you are sharing with. Jesus did something for you that no one else can ever, will ever, and doesn't even want to do. He saved you from Satan's destruction and replaced it with beauty. If that doesn't give you something exciting to tell others, honestly, I don't know what will.

In Acts 3, Peter and John were going up to the temple for prayer. Then this happened:

And a man who had been lame from his mother's womb was being carried along, whom they used to set down every day at the gate of the temple which is called Beautiful, in order to beg alms of those who were entering the temple. 3 When he saw Peter and John about to go into the temple, he began asking to receive alms. 4 But Peter, along with John, fixed his gaze on him and said, "Look at us!" 5 And he began to give them his attention, expecting to receive something from them. 6 But Peter said, "I do not possess silver and gold, but what I do have I give to you: In the name of Jesus Christ the Nazarene—walk!" 7 And seizing him by the right hand, he raised him up; and immediately his feet and his ankles were strengthened.

8 With a leap he stood upright and began to walk; and he entered the temple with them, walking and leaping and praising God. 9 And all the people saw him walking and praising God; 10 and they were taking note of him as being the one who used to sit at the Beautiful Gate of the temple to beg alms, and they were filled with wonder and amazement at what had happened to him.

I love to picture this man in my mind. Since his birth, he had never walked a step before, ever in his life. Now, in an instant, he was leaping, walking, and praising God. THAT kind of physical healing is like what God did for your soul. Before, you were spiritually lame. Now you have the ability to soar, full of joy and life! Take this man's example and go tell others what Jesus did for you!

A COMMISSION

I'd like to commission you on your journey with Scripture that has meant a lot to me over my years of ministry. This is my prayer for you, my evangelistic friend, as you go out into the world to make disciples of all the nations.

I solemnly charge you in the presence of God and of Christ Jesus, who is to judge the living and the dead, and by His appearing and His kingdom: preach the word; be ready in season and out of season; reprove, rebuke, exhort, with great patience and instruction. For the time will come when they will not endure sound doctrine; but wanting to have their ears tickled, they will accumulate for themselves teachers in accordance to their own desires, and will turn away their ears from the truth and will turn aside to myths. But you, be sober in all things, endure hardship, do the work of an evangelist, fulfill your ministry.

2 Timothy 4:1-5

Questions for Group Discussion:

Always begin your small group time with prayer.

1. Who in your life are the "works in progress"? As you've been living out the example of a Christian lifestyle have you ever given them the chance to make a decision to follow Christ? Would you? Why or why not?

2. Talk in your group about the potential "Timothys" that you can develop a discipleship relationship with. If you've had a discipleship partner before, talk about your experiences.

3. Where do you find it most difficult to shine your light? Why?

4. Following this final lesson, I have provided you with the lyrics to some songs that I think can touch your heart as you seek to be more evangelistic. Read them as a group. If you can, get the songs and listen to them. Journal any imagery or thoughts God brings to mind as you reflect.

5. Also following this final lesson are some additional evangelism stories from my personal experience. Take some time to read them and share what you learn from them.

SONGS

Mend Me

New Year's Eve, and this is what I see
Staring at these faces staring back at me
Sometimes insecure, but I know your love is pure

I am broken — mend me
Over backwards — bending
for the love you're sending

All the places that I've been
Still I can't escape this life of sin
What I want to do I don't do
And what I do I don't want to do

I am broken — mend me
Over backwards — bending
for the love you're sending

Days have come and days have gone
And still I'm under siege
Everyday decisions made for which side to alleige
Sometimes I just sit and cry for words I can't erase
All I have in this world is the promise of your grace

... You made the universe
And you can mend me

Music has always played an important role in my life. From my earliest recollections of my mom, blaring Phantom of the Opera as she twirled around our kitchen; to my days of playing and singing in a rock band; to the awesome privilege God gave me to serve as road pastor to many mainstream Christan artists, I can honestly say that music is one of the ways God ministers to my soul.

The lyrics of the songs on the next couple of pages are ones I find moving, especially in light of the subject of our study. The artists have given me permission to print these words, and for that I am extremely grateful.

Read them, look these songs up on the artists' websites, play them, let the words speak to you as you consider your commission as an evangelist.

Artist: Big Tent Revival (www.bigtentrevival.com)
© 1996 Ardent Christian Music. Used with permission.

Basics of Life

We've turned the page, for a new day has dawned
We've re-arranged what is right and what's wrong
Somehow we've drifted so far from the truth
That we can't get back home
Where are the virtues that once gave us light
Where are the morals that governed our lives
Someday we all will awake and look back
Just to find what we've lost

We need to get back to the basics of life
A heart that is pure and a love that is blind
A faith that is fervently grounded in Christ
The hope that endures for all times
These are the basics, we need to get back to the basics of life

The newest rage is to reason it out
Just meditate and you can overcome every doubt
After all man is a God, they say
God is no longer alive
But I still believe in the old rugged cross
And I still believe there is hope for the lost
And I know the rock of all ages will stand
Through changes of time

We've let the darkness invade us too long
We've got to turn the tide
Oh and we need the passion that burned long ago
To come and open our eyes
There's no room for compromise

Artist: 4HIM (www.4Him.net)
© 1997 Universal Music Publishing Group. Used with permission.

MORE STORIES OF SALVATION

THE NURSE'S STORY

Traveling across the country ministering to musicians and their crews was extremely rewarding. Not only did I get to see the backside of an industry I had passion for, as I helped those men and women, I got to know some amazing people, and lifelong friends. The downside is long nights sleeping on buses, being away from family for extended stretches of time, and occasionally the food options aren't so great.

At one venue, some of the band members and I had no choice but to go into a McDonald's for some grub. In front of us in line was a woman, wearing nurse's scrubs.

I leaned forward and asked her, "Are you a nurse?"

"Yes," she replied hesitantly.

"So, if I get sick, you could help me?" I asked.

"Well, it depends on what is wrong," she answered.

I said to her, "But God has given you some ability to help me if I was sick, right?"

"I suppose so," she said, not sure where I was going with my question.

"Can you help me with something else?" I went on. "Can you tell me how to get to heaven?"

Her face showed surprise, and she was speechless. I'm sure she'd never been asked that question.

I said, "You have the ability to help others when they are sick. Let me share with you what God has shared with me."

"Hang on a second," she said. She ordered her food. Then, in the middle of a crowded McDonald's I began to tell her what Jesus did for me. She got her food (to-go, as she had to get back to work) and I walked with her, continuing to tell her about Jesus. The band I was with followed us too, making us a bit of a parade. By the time we got to her car, I was at the part about why Jesus's love allows us access into heaven. I looked at her and said, "Can I ask you one more question? Is there any reason why you couldn't accept Christ today in your life so that one day you will enter the gates of heaven?"

She said she would like to ask Christ into her life. Everyone gathered around and we prayed. I invited her to the event that evening. Five bands played, and I spoke, sharing the gospel again. Afterward, as we were standing around talking, that woman came and found me.

"My name is Renee," she said. "I'm the woman from McDonald's."

"I remember," I said.

"I wanted to thank you. At first, when you started talking to me, I thought that you were a little crazy," she said.

I smiled. "Thanks, I get that a lot."

"But after seeing what took place tonight, I realize that I truly meant what I prayed."

I said, "Thank you for letting me know that."

I gave her advice as to how she could build on the decision she made. I instructed her to find a Bible-believing church and to tell the pastor that she is new to the faith, so that he can help her grow in her knowledge of who Jesus is.

THE WOODSTOCK STORY

In July 1999 I loaded up my car and drove to Rome, New York, where I intended to evangelize during the Woodstock 99 music festival. Because of my connections, I had credentials to move throughout all of the venues freely. It was an amazing experience. As you can imagine, parking was ridiculous and people were being bussed in from different places in the area. Concession prices were also ridiculous, but people could bring food in from outside the venue.

To provide people with practical and spiritual help, I decided to hand out special fliers. On one side was printed a map of the area, with parking and food options marked clearly. On the other side was a spiritual roadmap that showed two roads: one to heaven, and one to hell. The map explained how to get to heaven through salvation by Jesus Christ.

Along with my maps, I handed out different colored Mardi Gras type beads, as a bonus to those who stopped to talk to me. People began seeking me out as the "Bead Man." I was more than happy to share my beads and share Jesus. Even some of the bands playing requested me to give them some beads to throw from the stage. I didn't let them. My intent was to personally hand those beads over to people as I shared what Jesus did for them.

A number of years later, I was traveling in south Florida. I stopped at a convenience store, and I noticed a lady getting into her car. She had some Mardi Gras beads hanging from her rearview mirror.

"Nice Mardi Gras beads," I said, casually.

"Thanks, my daughter got those when she was at Woodstock 99," she said.

"You're kidding," I said. I stopped walking. "I was at Woodstock 99."

She said, "My daughter is inside getting some drinks for us."

When her daughter came out, the mom said to her, "Hey this guy was at Woodstock 99 too."

The girl started to speak, but then took a closer look at me.

"Mom, that's the bead guy," she said. "That's the guy who gave me the beads and the tract."

The girl told me that when she got home from the concert, she looked more closely at the map to heaven I handed out. She said that in the quiet of her bedroom, she prayed the prayer that was printed on the map and asked Jesus to come into her life. She thanked me for being there that day and for handing her the map to heaven. Together, she and her mom shared what Jesus was doing in their lives.

    Sometimes, we embark on a big journey, like traveling more than 800 miles to hand out beads and gospel tracts, and we never know what impact they have. Other times, God gives us a blessing, a great big hug, to let us know we made a difference through our efforts. That was what running into that woman and her daughter were for me that day. A big old hug from God saying, "See? Your evangelism matters."

THE ROCKET SCIENTIST'S STORY

This will probably come as no surprise to you, but I like to observe the people around me. I watch their movements, I listen to what they say, I try and allow God space to reveal things about them to me that I can use to initiate conversation, if the opportunity arises.

While traveling on a plane to Brazil, I took notice of the man seated across the aisle from me. From the way he was groomed, the type of clothes he wore, and the manner in which he carried himself, I got the impression that this guy was well put-together. He looked smart.

During the flight I asked him why he was traveling to Brazil.

"Are you going for work or for vacation?" I asked.

"A little of both," he replied.

"Oh, what do you do?" I probed.

"I'm a rocket scientist," he said. I have to admit, I was shocked. I even made a rocket scientist joke. We chatted for a bit and then he asked me what I did.

"I'm an evangelist," I stated.

"Interesting," he said. (I get that response a lot.)

As we continued talking I asked him a lot of questions about himself and his work, looking for places I could interject spiritual components to our discussion. When I asked about his experience with church, he vaguely replied that his work schedule didn't afford him too many chances to do things like church.

When the flight was over, we collected our things and I wished him well on his trip. Brazilian officials require everyone to remain silent and somber as you travel through the customs line. They even take your picture as you go through the turnstile.

I got through customs and started to exit the airport to get a cab so I could go to my hotel. From behind me I heard someone call, "Hey! Hey!"

I turned around, and rocket scientist man was chasing me down.

He said, "Do you have a few minutes? I want to talk to you about something. You were talking to me about Christ and how to get to heaven. Can you just share a little bit more about that with me to help me understand? I believe this is something I should do in my life."

I explained, in the most basic terms I could, what Jesus did for him and how to accept Christ.

He listened and then declared, "I want to do this. I want to accept Jesus into my life."

When I started to pray with him I took his right hand and I placed my left hand on his shoulder. In the middle of the chaotic airport, I prayed. He repeated back what I said, as he asked Jesus to come into his life. When we finished, he grabbed a hold of me and hugged me very tightly. He said, "Thank you."

"I hope you have a blessed time on your trip," I said.

"I believe this will be the best trip I've ever had in my life," he affirmed.

We exchanged contact information and kept in touch for a while. I sent him a Bible and other resources on how he could grow spiritually.

What God showed me through this experience is that even a rocket scientist needs to hear the basics of faith. We cannot assume that anyone's worldly credentials make them any further along spiritually than anyone else. We all start out as spiritual newborns.

YOUR STORY

What Jesus Did Bible Study — David Soesbee

Your Story

What Jesus Did Bible Study — David Soesbee

Your Story

EVANGELIST IN PROGRESS

Your story didn't end when you accepted Christ. You are in the "still changing" phase, where you will remain until Jesus calls you home. Just as I shared with you throughout this book the stories of salvation that God let me be a part of, and the things I learned that work and what doesn't work, you need to record the stories you are part of. You need to record the things God shows you as you evangelize.

Use these last few pages to start that recording. My prayer, though, is that God gives you so many stories of His glory in action that you fill this book and 7 more like it!

PEOPLE I'VE SHARED WITH

What Jesus Did Bible Study — David Soesbee

PRAYERS AND GOD'S ANSWERS

WHERE I'VE SEEN GOD'S HAND AT WORK

Evangelist in Progress

ABOUT THE AUTHOR

David Soesbee is an evangelist in every sense of the word. God gave David a vision and a passion for the lost that compels him to tell others about Jesus.

David is a graduate of Fruitland Bible College, where he earned his Associate's Degree in 1996. He was ordained in 1998. David received a Master's Degree from Carolina University of Theology.

Throughout his ministry, God has given David the privilege of ministering in a wide variety of situations and unique settings. The doors that the Lord has opened for him have allowed him to stand before seemingly "untouchables" and declare the gospel of Christ.

David served as a chaplain to the NASCAR community for 12 years. He has spent many months on the road with Christian and non-Christian music bands as their road pastor. He provided personal ministry at the past 5 Summer Olympic games to athletes and their families, encouraging and building up the host city communities. He has preached the gospel in 51 countries (and counting!), and he has presented the gospel in some of the wackiest, most creative ways possible. Whether he is talking to the person in line at the grocery store or to a mega-rockstar, he never waivers in taking the opportunity to tell others about Jesus.

What Jesus Did ministry is focused on equipping and encouraging the body of Christ to grow in their passion for evangelism. David speaks at conferences, church events, youth revivals, men's groups, and workshops. What Jesus Did has one goal: to get the whole world talking about What Jesus Did.

David and his wife, Kimberly, have three incredibly talented, beautiful children. They live in the Dallas / Ft. Worth, Texas area. You can reach David to book speaking dates through www.WhatJesusDid.org.

www.ingramcontent.com/pod-product-compliance
Lightning Source LLC
Chambersburg PA
CBHW080440110426
42743CB00016B/3221